AN INTRODUCTION TO
COACHING SKILLS

AN INTRODUCTION TO
COACHING SKILLS
A PRACTICAL GUIDE

CHRISTIAN
VAN NIEUWERBURGH

SAGE

Los Angeles | London | New Delhi
Singapore | Washington DC

Los Angeles | London | New Delhi
Singapore | Washington DC

SAGE Publications Ltd
1 Oliver's Yard
55 City Road
London EC1Y 1SP

SAGE Publications Inc.
2455 Teller Road
Thousand Oaks, California 91320

SAGE Publications India Pvt Ltd
B 1/I 1 Mohan Cooperative Industrial Area
Mathura Road
New Delhi 110 044

SAGE Publications Asia-Pacific Pte Ltd
3 Church Street
#10-04 Samsung Hub
Singapore 049483

Editor: Kate Wharton
Editorial assistant: Laura Walmsley
Production editor: Rachel Burrows
Marketing manager: Tamara Navaratnam
Cover design: Lisa Harper
Typeset by: C&M Digitals (P) Ltd, Chennai, India
Printed and bound in Great Britain by Ashford
Colour Press Ltd

© Christian van Nieuwerburgh, 2014

First published 2014

Library of Congress Control Number: 2013940312

British Library Cataloguing in Publication data

A catalogue record for this book is available from
the British Library

MIX
Paper from
responsible sources
FSC
www.fsc.org   FSC® C011748

ISBN 978-1-4462-6020-3
ISBN 978-1-4462-6021-0 (pbk)

To Cathia and Christian, with my love and admiration

CONTENTS

ABOUT THE AUTHOR

Christian is a well-respected executive coach, internationally-recognised academic and sought-after consultant.

He is a Programme Leader and Senior Lecturer within the Coaching Psychology programmes at the University of East London, one of the world's leading centres for the postgraduate study of coaching. He lectures on a number of MSc programmes in the School of Psychology, undertakes ground-breaking research and international collaborations in coaching and supervises academic dissertations.

Seen as an international authority in the field of coaching, he has been invited to speak at conferences in the US, the UK, Europe, Australia and the Middle East. He regularly presents on the topics of coaching, motivation, mental toughness and leadership. Christian has written a number of peer-reviewed journal articles and chapters about coaching.

Christian is particularly passionate about the power of coaching in educational settings. He is the editor of *Coaching in Education: Getting Better Results for Students, Educators and Parents* (2012), which is now one of the key textbooks in the field. Through his consultancy, the International Centre for Coaching in Education (ICCE), Christian delivers training, consultancy, coaching and professional development programmes to schools, colleges and universities in the UK and abroad. He is motivated by the idea of creating coaching cultures for learning which allow students to purposefully and confidently pursue their aspirations.

Christian defines himself as an engaged academic practitioner, committed to the useful interplay of theory, research and practice. Students, delegates, clients and peers describe him as an inspirational educator and empowering coach.

Twitter: @ChristianvN
Email: christian@icce.uk.com

PREFACE

Welcome to *An Introduction to Coaching Skills: A Practical Guide*. This is a book that I have genuinely enjoyed writing. I have spent many fruitful days thinking about the intended reader, so I'm very excited that you are now reading it!

In a coaching conversation that took place about seven years ago, I remember saying to my coach that I wanted to transform my professional life so that I could turn more of my attention and energy towards coaching. As a result of that conversation, I now spend most of my professional life coaching others, training people to become coaches and working with organisations interested in establishing coaching cultures.

I have learned a tremendous amount in the process of writing this book. Firstly, when there is an essential connection between learning and living, life seems to be more fulfilling. I worked on this book using time that would otherwise be spent at work or at home with the family. It seemed to sit comfortably in both domains and gave me permission to be thinking about coaching almost all the time! Secondly, it's become clearer to me that becoming coaches allows us to be engaged with learning and human growth, tapping into our natural tendency to be lifelong learners. Finally, as I worked hard to convey my knowledge and experiences of coaching, I have come to appreciate how there is such a rich tapestry which brings together learning from formal education, from other coaches and from my own coaching practice. Despite my best efforts, not everyone will be acknowledged in this book. I am very grateful to my teachers, coaches, students and clients for sharing their thoughts and insights with me.

Most importantly, I have had a chance to explore the idea that coaching is both complex and simple. Its complexity rests in the richness of human relationships and the ways in which people try to help one another. And yet, at the same time, effective coaching is simply a lived demonstration of the most positive elements of what it is to be human. Those of us who embrace coaching find that it rekindles our curiosity, deepens our respect for others and sharpens our appreciation of the complexity and beauty of human nature.

I am passionate about facilitating learning, and this book is an attempt to support your development. To be as helpful as possible in this regard, I have worked with my wonderful publishers and tapped into the generosity of colleagues and students to give you the resources you need. There are videos of coaching practice, short introductions to the chapters, suggested activities, a Companion Website and a MobileStudy site. In addition, I have interwoven real examples from my own coaching practice into the text. Within the bounds of confidentiality and respecting the anonymity of clients, I have included some 'stories from practice' which are based on real experiences.

I hope you will discover, like I did, that learning to become a coach can have a positive impact on all aspects of your life. As an example, I'd like to share a true story with you.

For the last few years, I have been working in London for most of the week, driving or taking the train back to my home in the countryside on weekends. On a good day, it's a three-hour drive from the University to our house in Warwickshire. On one of these journeys home in November, I pulled into a service station just off the motorway, about halfway to my destination. It was about 8:00pm, so already quite dark. I parked my car, locked it and started walking to the coffee shop for a hot drink. A voice called out 'Good evening, brother'. Glancing to my left, I saw a man looking out of the window of a small green car. 'Good evening,' I replied. He peered out of his car, looking embarrassed. 'Brother, can I speak to you?' he asked politely. Slightly on my guard, I went over to the car. He told me that he had been having a very bad day. He had driven his brother to Heathrow Airport in the morning. Due to some difficulties with excess baggage and airport security, he ended up having to give his brother all the cash he had. Now, on his way back home, he was out of fuel and had no access to money or a credit card. He had asked the petrol station attendant to call his wife so that she could pay for his fuel over the phone using a credit card, but apparently there was some regulation that meant this was not possible. He asked if I could help him in some way. At that moment, a slight feeling of doubt crept over me. He told me where he worked in his hometown and offered to give me his mobile phone number. My personal value of helping people when they are in need competed with cynical thoughts about the credibility of the situation. However, I decided that I should behave in a way that was in line with my values. I took out the only £20 note in my wallet and gave it to him. 'Here you are,' I said. He thanked me and promised to pay me back as soon as he was paid on the following Tuesday. 'Give me your name and address, and I will post you a cheque on Tuesday,' he promised. Instead of giving him my address, I simply gave him my mobile phone number. I told him not to worry about the cheque for now, but to focus on getting home. 'When you've been paid on Tuesday, just give me a call and I'll let you know how to get the money back to me', I said. He thanked me for being a 'brother in need', and drove off. I had decided that if he did call on the following Tuesday, I would tell him that he could keep the £20 as a gift.

Before I learned to become a coach, I would have been much more cynical and less trusting. I probably would not have spoken to this person, let alone lend him money at a petrol station. However, in the moment, I consciously decided to give the person the benefit of the doubt. As I sipped on my coffee as I drove home, I felt good about having done the 'right'thing. You may already have guessed that I didn't get a call on Tuesday. In fact, I never heard from that person again. But I'd like to think that if a similar thing happened at a motorway services in future, I would, once again, give a stranger in need the benefit of the doubt. Becoming a coach has helped me to be less judgemental and more trusting.

I hope you find this book valuable and enjoy becoming a coach as much as I have!

ACKNOWLEDGEMENTS

I consider myself to be incredibly fortunate to be surrounded by supportive and encouraging people. What a wonderful opportunity to note my gratitude to some of them!

Firstly, I'd like to register my appreciation to the wonderfully energizing and dedicated group of students at the University of East London (UEL) who I have the pleasure of working with every year. Their commitment to coaching, their challenging questions and their desire to support others is always inspirational.

Secondly, the School of Psychology at UEL is my home in London. My colleagues in the Coaching Psychology Unit, Dr Ho Chung Law, William Pennington and Julia Yates are a wonderful and supportive team to be part of. I appreciate their enthusiasm about coaching and clear focus on the student experience at UEL. Julia has been particularly supportive of this project, and features as a coach on some of the video clips! As a School, we are well supported by an effective administrative team. I'd like to particularly thank Susy Ajith, Kevin Head, Marika Hemming, Shaila Karim, Luke Madden, Will Munday, Andrew Talbot and Michael Wozniak for helping to keep me in the good books of the institution! Academic colleagues such as Prof. Mark Davies, Prof. Irvine Gersch, Dr Carla Gibbes, Dr Kate Hefferon, Mark Holloway, Dr Ashok Jansari, Gordon Jinks, Prof. Rachel Mulvey, Dr Chris Pawson, Dr Nash Popovic, Dr Amanda Roberts and Dr Dori Yusef (among others) create an energizing space for learning and research within the School of Psychology. I am particularly grateful for the unwavering and valuable support of Dr Aneta Tunariu, Head of Subject for Psychological Interventions at UEL.

Beyond the University, I am privileged to work with outstanding people, such as Liz Hall, Jane Harders, Glyn Owen, Doug Strycharczyk and Bob Thomson in the UK. Each of these people has been generous in their support and engagement with my passion for coaching. It is also my good fortune to work with inspirational coaches and educators abroad. Each of the following people have inspired me to broaden my horizons: Raja al-Laho of Gulf Lead Consultants in Kuwait, John Campbell of the Growth Coaching International in Australia, Dr Anthony Grant, at the University of Sydney, Dr Suzy Green of the Positivity Institute in Australia, Dr Jim Knight at the University of Kansas in the US, and Dr Steve Zolezzi at Knox Grammar School in Australia. All of these people deserve my sincere thanks. They make my life more exciting!

I would not be doing what I am doing now if it weren't for a key group of educators and colleagues who have believed in me and supported me. Dr Martin Wiggins, my PhD supervisor, was a model academic and world leader in the study of Elizabethan and Jacobean drama. Sue Herdman, Mary Johnson and Miles Tandy have been valuable colleagues and wonderful teachers, showing me the art of facilitation. David Love, who launched me onto the path of becoming a coach, demonstrated to me the 'way of being' that I discuss in this book. Dr Jonathan Passmore acted as a mentor and coach to me as I found my feet within the world of academia.

I love to work in schools and often ask delegates at conferences or participants at workshops to remember an educator who had a significant positive impact on them. Invariably, when I ask what made the particular educator memorable, participants report that the person 'believed in me'. Again, I have been unusually lucky in this regard. In the sixth grade of the American Community School (ACS) of Beirut, Donald Corsette discovered a good kid who could be rebellious at times. He transformed my educational experience from that moment onwards. Catherine Bashshur, the head teacher of ACS, gave me the benefit of the doubt on more than one occasion. At the American University of Beirut, Dr Jean-Marie Cook encouraged me to pursue a PhD in Elizabethan Drama. I didn't believe that I would be able to do it. But she did. And I will be forever grateful to Dr George Khairallah who was a natural sage. On the first day of my Shakespeare module at AUB, George stood on one leg, with a set of worry beads as a crown, for the entire lesson. He taught me the power of 'A-ha!' moments.

I have been excited about this book from the outset. Kate Wharton, my visionary commissioning editor, has been a steadfast support and champion for this book. Laura Walmsley, editorial assistant, has kept me connected to the project, nudging me along as needed. Rachel Burrows, managing senior production editor, and Martin Noble, copy editor, were very professional, efficiently turning a massive word-processed document into an amazing book!

My colleague at UEL, Dan Bowden, deserves a special mention for professionally filming and editing all of the video clips. He has been a source of expertise and wonderful good humour. A number of current and former students kindly volunteered to undertake coaching while being filmed. Their generosity and trust in the process has meant that this book is greatly enriched by access to glimpses of real coaching sessions. Many of the participants are now coaches in their own right and yet agreed to be filmed as coachees for the sake of this project. I am deeply grateful to Zaydon Alayasa, Jane Ayres, Greg Ette, Karen Foy, Grace Graham, Katie Heath, Ian McIntosh, Michelle Pritchard, Dionne Spencer, Matt Sheerin, Trish Smith, Carol Stewart and Astrid Weinmann. Thanks are also due to other current and former students who volunteered to be filmed but could not attend on the filming days.

What makes my executive coaching, student coaching and consultancy work so rewarding is the opportunity to work with people who are committed to their own development and wish to pursue their dreams and aspirations. I appreciate what a privilege this is. I'd therefore like to thank all the people (adults and young people) that I have had the opportunity to work with or coach.

I would like to conclude my acknowledgements by thanking my friends and family. Igor Djordjevic and Jawad Maatouk are childhood friends who have continued to provide encouragement and good times. The Jenainati family has accepted me as one of their own. I am especially thankful to Riad and Hoda, Amin, Suzy, Zeina, Hani, Natalie, Charbel and all of my cousins and nieces for their love and kindness. My father, Arthur John van Nieuwerburgh, lived his life to the full and would have wanted me to do the same. At the age of 87, my mother, Tsuyu Tsuchida, is a model of resilience and generosity. My wife Cathia is the love of my life and the best partner I could ever imagine. My son, Christian Arthur van Nieuwerburgh, is an admirable, caring and thoughtful young man. I'd like to thank my friends and family for allowing me to flourish by believing in me and allowing me the space and time to follow my heart.

GUIDED TOUR OF THE BOOK

The aim of this book is to be as helpful as possible to you as you learn to coach. With this in mind, there are a number of additional practical resources incorporated within the text. It is recommended that you engage with these to support your learning and build confidence in your newly acquired skills and abilities.

Companion website

This book is accompanied by a Companion Website featuring over 70 videos of live coaching sessions, chapter summaries and activities explained that will help to elucidate certain elements of good coaching practice. The short clips, identifiable by this symbol in the margin and found at the following link **www.sagepub.co.uk/vannieuwerburgh**, show brief introductions to chapters and activities or edited segments of live coaching sessions. We have chosen the keyhole image as a marker of these video clips because some of them provide an opportunity to peek into the coaching space. As most coaching conversations are confidential, these video clips represent a relatively rare opportunity to observe real coaching taking place. The clips have been selected to demonstrate the key skills and processes of a coaching conversation. It is not essential to view these video clips, but many novice coaches find these to be a very helpful additional resource.

Watch Videos 0.1 and 0.2 to see a brief introduction to the book and coaching videos.

In addition to the videos, the Companion Website features coaching resources and other additional materials that you may find useful.

MobileStudy

You can also study on the go with the SAGE MobileStudy site. Simply scan any QR code at the beginning of each chapter to download these videos and additional resources to your mobile.

Activity

Practical activities that encourage reflection and the consolidation of learning are identified throughout the text. Most of these should only take a few minutes of your time. Of course, it is possible to skip over these but your investment of time in these brief activities is likely to lead to a better learning experience. See Video 0.3 for an introduction to the activities.

FIND OUT MORE

Periodically, there are suggestions for further reading, additional online resources or recommended websites. This will allow you to go into as much depth as is helpful about topics of interest.

Story from Practice

Many of the skills and processes presented in this book are supported by real stories from coaching practice. These may help your learning by providing you with case studies and useful anecdotes. As you will discover, confidentiality is an essential part of the coaching process. All of the stories presented in this book are taken from my own experiences. For this reason, some details have been changed in cases where it may have otherwise been possible for a person or organisation to be identified. While some details relating to identifiable factors have been changed, none of the significant coaching-related events has been altered, and therefore these are 'true' stories based on real experiences. I have worked with clients and organisations in the UK and internationally over many years, and therefore I believe that no clients or organisations will be identifiable. Where I was concerned about issues of confidentiality or anonymity, I have shared the case studies with those involved before including them in this book.

SNAPSHOT

While this book is intentionally focused on the *practice* of coaching, the text is underpinned by reference to coaching-related theory and research. Sometimes it is helpful to provide a snapshot or a brief explanation of such theories or relevant research. These are presented in boxes within the text and can provide readers with additional helpful information.

What About You?

Throughout the text, you will notice 'What about you?' questions. These are invitations for you to reflect on your response to a particular theory or practice. Learning to become a coach is as much about increasing your own self-awareness as it is about studying about processes, tools and techniques. Hopefully, you will find some of these questions challenging or thought-provoking.

LIST OF VIDEOS ON THE COMPANION WEBSITE

PART ONE
CONTEXT

1
FIRST THINGS FIRST

Welcome

Welcome to the start of an exciting learning journey! This book will be an important part of your development as a coach – but not the only element. Like many other forms of personal and professional development, coaching requires practice and intentional reflection. On the one hand, by the time you have read the entire book, watched the related video clips and completed the suggested activities, you will be ready to coach others. On the other hand, learning the 'way of being' discussed in this book is a lifetime endeavour. Importantly and fortunately, if you have chosen this book for yourself, it will be an enjoyable endeavour. By embarking on your own learning journey, it is very likely that you will inspire others to do the same.

What is coaching?

Before going any further, it is important that we agree a working definition of the word 'coaching'. The fact that you are reading this suggests that you have a good idea of what it means already. And in many ways, what you believe it means is more important than the tentative definition proposed below.

One-sentence definition   Activity

Here is the first activity! Take a few minutes to jot down your own one-sentence definition of coaching. Try to restrict yourself to just one sentence. Once you've completed this, make a note of the sentence and compare your definition with those presented below.

At the time of writing, there is no legal definition of coaching. This fact is often cited as a weakness for the 'profession' of coaching. There is little doubt that the very fact that anyone can call anything they do 'coaching' can be confusing and potentially unhelpful for others who call themselves 'coaches'. At the same time, this allows for a certain freedom for each coach to define her practice in a way that is meaningful to herself and her clients.

FIND OUT MORE   The history of coaching

The most comprehensive outline of the foundations and history of coaching can be found in a seminal book by Dr Vikki Brock entitled *Sourcebook of Coaching History*.

Over the last 20 years, a number of key definitions have been proposed. (See **www.sagepub. co.uk/vannieuwerburgh** for a more comprehensive list of definitions.) A few notable definitions are listed below:

> 'The art of facilitating the performance, learning and development of another.' (Downey, 2003: 21)

This definition is interesting because of its characterisation of coaching as an 'art'. This is in contrast with many that suggest that there is a science of coaching. For example, I teach on a 'coaching psychology' programme within a school of psychology – and psychology has fought hard to establish its credentials as a science. Having said this, I believe that coaching is both an art and a science. In this book, we will consider both angles. The tools, techniques and processes may be seen as more *scientific* whereas the 'way of being' section leans more towards the idea of coaching as an *art*. There has been an increasing amount of credible research into coaching to provide evidence for its effectiveness. This will be brought into the discussion lightly, when appropriate.

Downey's definition goes on to suggest that coaching should focus on performance, learning and development. This emphasis on performance is a feature of much of the early literature on coaching, perhaps because of the desire of early adopters to convince others of its suitability in the workplace.

> 'Unlocking people's potential to maximise their own performance. It is helping them to learn rather than teaching them.' (Whitmore, 2009: 11)

Like Downey, Whitmore highlights the performance-enhancing nature of coaching. This is probably one of the best-known definitions in the field and it often captures the imagination of people wishing to become coaches. It suggests that every person has the potential within herself and the wording implies that the coachee must take responsibility for maximising her own performance. The second sentence is less frequently quoted, perhaps because it is more controversial. Whitmore explicitly juxtaposes coaching (helping people to learn) with teaching (telling people what they need to know).

'Coaching is a method of work-related learning that relies primarily on one-to-one conversations.' (de Haan, 2008b: 19)

In a definition that has a clear bias towards executive coaching, de Haan proposes that conversations should focus on work-related learning and development. His use of the phrase 'primarily on one-to-one conversations' alludes to the existence of 'group' or 'team' coaching. This book will focus on coaching as a one-to-one relationship, which is the foundation of powerful conversations. Many of the skills, tools and techniques you develop as you learn to become a coach will be immediately transferable to other aspects of your life. Furthermore, in principle, the skills of coaching are the same, regardless of the context in which they are used. This book will help you to develop your ability to coach in any arena – within organisations, as a life coach, within educational or health settings or as part of a leadership role.

'[Coaching may be defined as] a human development process that involves structured, focused interaction and the use of appropriate strategies, tools and techniques to promote desirable and sustainable change for the benefit of the coachee and potentially for other stakeholders'. (Cox, Bachkirova and Clutterbuck, 2010: 1)

This definition is more comprehensive, recognising the important role of coaching as part of a developmental process. Sustainability of the change achieved during coaching is picked out as a significant consideration. There is acknowledgement that there may be benefits to 'other stakeholders' in addition to benefits for the coachee. In executive coaching situations, it is hoped that both the coachee and her organisation will profit from coaching sessions.

Our definition of coaching

Considering the quotes above, it can be said that there is some variation in definitions, but the essence of coaching is captured by Bresser and Wilson who hone in on the notion that it is about 'empowering people by facilitating self-directed learning, personal growth and improved performance' (2010: 10). There seems to be broad agreement in the literature that coaching:

(a) is a managed conversation that takes place between two people;
(b) aims to support sustainable change to behaviours or ways of thinking;
(c) focuses on learning and development.

Coaching is a conversational process and a set of easily learned techniques. The skills needed to be a coach, you possess already: the ability to listen to others, to ask questions and to summarise. From here onwards, it is simply a case of honing these skills in order to effectively facilitate one-to-one conversations with others. If you are reading this book, it is likely that you already possess an essential and necessary attribute: a desire to support others to achieve more of their potential.

And yet this simplicity does not prevent coaching from being a powerful and rewarding activity. In some cases, it can be life-changing – for you as well as the coachee! This comes from another factor that will be discussed in this book: the relationship between the coach and the coachee.

Coaching and mentoring

Many words, spoken and written, have been expended trying to tease out the differences between coaching and mentoring. As I hope you will discover as you read through this book, the key skills, many of the approaches and the need for a particular 'way of being' are similar in both activities. In an attempt to distinguish the two approaches, Passmore (2010) suggests some differentiating factors. Firstly, he proposes that coaching is more formal than mentoring. According to Passmore, mentoring tends to be an informal arrangement between two people. Compared to mentoring, coaching is seen to be a shorter-term engagement. Coaching is considered a more appropriate intervention for skills or performance enhancement while mentoring is better suited to career development. It is proposed that the most significant difference between the two approaches is the need for a mentor to have a high level of expertise and knowledge about the topic being discussed. Bresser and Wilson (2010) helpfully highlight two factors which differentiate the approaches:

1. A mentor has 'experience in a particular field and imparts specific knowledge' while a coach does not necessarily have specialist experience in the field and does not impart knowledge (p. 22).
2. A mentor acts as an 'adviser, counsellor, guide, tutor, or teacher' while a coach's role is to 'assist coachees in uncovering their own knowledge and skills' and 'facilitate coachees in becoming their own advisers' (p. 22).

In addition to a shared set of skills, the intentions of coaches and mentors are often closely aligned – supporting others to achieve more of their goals and aspirations. Garvey, Stokes and Megginson agree that 'coaching and mentoring are essentially similar in nature' (2009: 27). Further, a piece of research into this question by Willis (2005) found that coaching and mentoring were similar activities with coaches and mentors sharing the same skills and practices.

As I have argued elsewhere (van Nieuwerburgh, 2012), the terminology is unimportant as long as it is recognised that both approaches can support people to develop their skills and performance while helping them to unlock their potential. For the purposes of this book, it may suffice to conclude that both approaches are broadly similar. Here, we are interested primarily in coaching.

How will this book help?

This book should help you in a number of ways. For some readers, the book may introduce completely new ideas and concepts. For others, it may reaffirm existing practices and behaviours.

Hopefully, all readers will find this book's focus on practice helpful. Ultimately, this book should give you the skills needed to be able to coach others and support you to feel more confident about your ability to do so effectively. To aid you in this process, this book provides a clear structure (outlined below) which starts with the key skills before focusing on a well-respected coaching process. This is followed by some practical techniques and tools that can be used during different stages of the coaching conversation. The section on 'Way of being' captures the 'art' element of coaching, and this is discussed once readers are familiar with the skills and process involved. You will be supported on your learning journey with a number of learning aids and a Companion Website (**www.sagepub.co.uk/vannieuwerburgh**) which will enhance the practical dimension to this book. Turn back to page xvi to remind yourself about what each of these additional practical resources has to offer.

Creating a reflective learning journal   Activity

Create an electronic or hard copy learning journal as a companion to this book. At various stages during your reading, journal entries will be suggested. In addition, it may be helpful to capture your own thoughts, reflections and questions as you read through this book.

In the first entry of your new reflective learning journal, note down your thoughts and feelings about the chapters which are described briefly below. A few bullet points will be sufficient for each chapter.

- What thoughts come to mind when you read the brief descriptions?
- What are you curious about as you read through the brief descriptions?
- How much are you looking forward to reading each chapter? Perhaps rate this on a scale of 1 (dreading the chapter) to 10 (cannot wait to read the chapter).

Chapter outlines

To give you a sense of what is to follow, here is a brief synopsis of every chapter. I would recommend that you read through the chapters in order first, but then use the brief descriptions below in future when you want to use this book as a reference as you start to coach others.

Context

1. First things first

This is the chapter you're reading. This provides an introduction to the book, an overview of the related resources and this brief overview of each chapter.

2. Becoming a coach

This chapter introduces the three elements of becoming an effective coach: having the necessary skills; knowing a coaching process and adopting an appropriate 'way of being'. Most readers will already have the necessary skills of coaching which are defined as 'listening to encourage thinking', 'asking powerful questions', 'summarising and paraphrasing' and 'giving and receiving feedback'. This book will support readers to strengthen and refine these skills. One of the key roles of the coach is to manage the conversation by facilitating a process. This can be done by learning and adopting one of many coaching models. These are easy to learn, and take practice to master. This book will present readers with a coaching process that they will be able to use straight away. Finally, the best coaches demonstrate a particular 'way of being'. This cannot be taught, but can be learned over time and with practice. If readers can develop all three elements, they will be able to confidently support others to achieve more of their potential.

Key coaching skills

3. Listening to encourage thinking

Listening is an underrated skill. When used effectively, listening can make people feel valued, respected and resourceful. Different levels of listening will be discussed. Particular approaches to active listening are explored. The premise of this chapter is that skilful listening can encourage others to think more creatively and positively.

4. Asking powerful questions

This chapter highlights the importance of using questions that have a purpose. The appropriate use of both open and closed questions will be considered. Four types of questions are proposed. There is a discussion of particular types of questions appropriate to specific coaching situations.

5. Summarising and paraphrasing

Summarising and paraphrasing play an important part in a coaching conversation. This chapter considers how best to 'play back' information to coachees. The importance of summarising or paraphrasing to demonstrate attentive listening is explained. The chapter provides some useful phrases for use during coaching.

6. Giving and receiving feedback

As coaching is about increasing self-awareness in the person being coached, the coach needs to know how to give helpful feedback. Providing high-quality, objective information to the person being coached can help to increase understanding of her situation. In addition, the coach needs to be able to positively accept feedback to improve her own practice.

The coaching process

7. The GROW model

This chapter begins this section by introducing a simple coaching process (GROW). The use of the GROW model (Whitmore, 2009) is discussed in relation to supporting people to change their behaviours. The GROW model is described in detail (with diagrams) and with sample questions for use in a behavioural context.

8. Beyond behaviour: exploring our thinking

Having described the GROW model in detail in the previous chapter, the way in which coaches can support the thinking processes of coachees is discussed. While many people seek coaching to change behaviour, more often the person being coached may need to change her way of thinking before sustained change in behaviour can take place. Reference will be made to the concept of the 'inner game' (Gallwey, 1974).

9. Using positive psychology

The field of positive psychology has much to offer coaches. A brief overview of the field is followed by some positive psychological interventions that may be helpful to coaches and coachees. The solution-focused coaching framework is presented as an alternative to the GROW model. It is a very effective, targeted coaching intervention.

Practical tools and techniques

10. Body language and emotional intelligence

This chapter discusses the role of body language and emotional intelligence in coaching conversations. The importance of remaining alert to body language (as additional 'data') is highlighted. Emotional intelligence (Salovey and Mayer, 1990) is also essential for a coach, as she will need to be aware of the emotions of the coachee as well as her own. By making educated guesses about how the person being coached is feeling, the coach is able to adapt her own behaviour accordingly.

11. Inspiring creativity: let's talk

For novice coaches, the 'Options' stage of the GROW model can be the most challenging. Three chapters propose a range of tools and techniques for increasing the creativity of the person being coached. The first of these chapters considers conversational approaches. Clear directions are provided for each of the activities.

12. Inspiring creativity: let's draw

Coaching is primarily a conversational tool. That is why it is sometimes helpful to include activities that might appeal to visual learners. Drawing is also a way of accessing new ideas or exploring things differently. A broad range of drawing and writing activities are explained.

13. Inspiring creativity: let's play

In addition to conversational and drawing activities, some coachees like to get more active during coaching sessions. It takes a bit more confidence on the part of the coach to 'play' during a coaching session but this is often a good way of generating new ideas and perspectives in a non-threatening way.

Way of being

14. Being human

The 'way of being' necessary for the most effective coaching cannot be *taught* in the traditional sense of the word. Instead, this can only be learned by people for whom it is important. This chapter describes the key attributes of the 'way of being' by outlining the person-centred approach to coaching and discussing a series of 'partnership principles'. The chapter concludes by providing some aspirational goals for coaches.

15. Inspiring others

Coaching is an ideal way of inspiring others to strive towards success. Coaches can do this through their coaching, but also in everyday life. This can be achieved by adopting a coaching approach. Some ways of doing this are suggested.

Conclusion

16. Reflecting on practice

This chapter suggests that coaching growth and maturity can be developed through reflective practice. This reflection can take place individually, in peer groups or during supervision. Becoming the best coach you can be is a lifelong endeavour. This chapter also discusses the importance of ethics in coaching and will help readers to start thinking about their future development as coaches. This chapter will suggest ways of continuing to develop your skills and 'way of being' through practice, formal learning opportunities and supervisory conversations.

My intention is to provide a resource that is both practical and evidence-based. While the focus remains securely on the skills, processes and 'way of being' needed in order to support *others*, I am confident that you will benefit personally and professionally from learning to become a coach. This view is supported by recent research that showed that students who were trained to become coaches (and subsequently coached other students) showed increases in levels of emotional intelligence (van Nieuwerburgh and Tong, 2013). These students reported that they had developed their own communication skills and felt that they had developed many transferable skills. Practising coaching can help you to develop the 'way of being' that can be particularly helpful in coaching as well as in everyday life, at work, at school, with friends and family. As you learn to become a coach, you will find that you start to listen more authentically to others, ask better questions and become better at building rapport and meaningful relationships. Whatever else we do, we need to remember that coaching is an intervention that has as its 'underlying and ever-present goal' the building of others' self-belief 'regardless of the content of the task or issue' (Whitmore, 2009: 19).

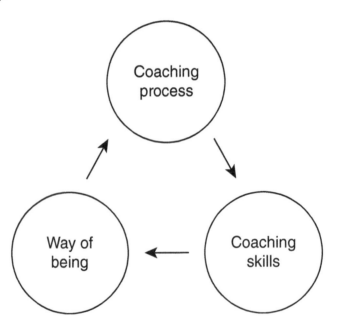

2
BECOMING A COACH

Figure 2.1 The three elements of effective coaching

Does a person learn *how to* coach or does she *become* a coach? This is an interesting question, and there are a number of different ways to address it. Many people learn to coach in a transactional way, focusing narrowly on the process. For example, I remember hearing some managers who had recently received coaching training discussing the idea of 'putting on a coaching hat' before starting to coach others. There is no doubt that this is possible. A person can 'do' coaching without 'being' a coach. However, if you are hoping to inspire others and support them to achieve great things, I believe that you have to *become* a coach.

To become a coach requires three areas of learning which will be covered in this book: a set of skills, a clear process and a 'way of being' (see Figure 2.1). The first two ('coaching skills' and 'coaching process') can be taught, and often form the basis of short training courses on coaching. I would argue, however, that simply knowing the skills and being able to follow a process will not guarantee successful outcomes. They allow a person to 'do' coaching. The third element is the most influential. Ironically, this element, which I shall refer to as a 'way of being', cannot be taught. However, the most effective coaches have a deep understanding and appreciation of all three elements.

The structure of this book is built on these foundations. We will start by building on your existing skills. If you are reading this text, you are very likely to possess the foundational skills already. It will simply be a case of honing or sharpening these skills so that you can use them for the specific purpose of coaching. Once we have discussed the necessary skills in some detail, we shall move on to a coaching process. In this case, we will be concentrating on one coaching process: the well-known and very effective GROW model (Whitmore, 2009). We will then look at additional approaches, tools and techniques that can supplement the GROW model. Once your skills are honed and the process has been learned, we will explore the concept of 'way of being'. Hopefully, you will be able to quickly develop the coaching-related skills and learn the GROW model. That will be the foundation of your coaching practice. Developing a 'way of being' is a lifelong journey. The good news is that the best way of developing a 'way of being' is through practising coaching and reflecting on your experiences.

As we start this journey, we should begin by being clear about what we are working towards. There are a number of different areas in which coaching is flourishing. This introductory book provides a firm foundation for your practice, whichever field you wish to practise in:

1. Executive coaching: Working in organisations with middle and senior leaders
2. Life coaching: Working with individuals on topics relating to their personal lives
3. Health coaching: Working with patients and health professionals
4. Coaching in education: Working with students, educators and parents
5. Career coaching: Working with professionals about their career development
6. Leadership coaching: Working with leaders in any profession or field

As you work your way through this book, you should be starting to think about which arena you would like to start with. If you are hoping to develop a coaching business, I would recommend starting by focusing on a niche area in which you are likely to have some credibility already.

SNAPSHOT   A 'typical' coaching session

Before the session

Pre-coaching session discussion (in person or over the telephone). Usually 10–20 minutes. This is an opportunity for you to introduce yourself to the coachee, agree a time and place for the first meeting and get an idea of the topic.

(Continued)

(Continued)

During the session

Coaching sessions are usually between 30 minutes and 2 hours in length. Approximate times below are based on a 2-hour session.

Small talk to build rapport (5 minutes)

The coach initiates a discussion which is unrelated to the coaching topic in order to put the coachee at ease and start the process of building rapport. In the UK, we like to talk about the weather!

Getting to know one another (10 minutes)

It can be helpful for the coach to introduce herself briefly. This is a good time to find out a little bit more about what the coachee does on a day-to-day basis, whether or not this relates directly to the coaching conversation. This is also the right time to agree a 'contract' about how the coaching will proceed. The importance of contracting for coaching conversations is covered in Chapter 7.

Setting goals (15 minutes)

In this section, the coach should support the coachee to identify the topic for the coaching conversation and some goals. This will be discussed in detail in the chapter about the GROW model (Chapter 7).

Talking about what is happening currently (20 minutes)

This is the part when the coachee should be doing most of the talking. The coach's role is to listen carefully while the coachee explains what is happening for her at the moment. The coach should ensure that the coachee focuses on her current reality *in relation to the goal* that she will have identified.

Exploring options (30 minutes)

Once the coachee has explained the current state of play in relation to her topic or self-selected goal, the coach should support the coachee to generate some possible ways forward. This is a very important part of the coaching conversation and we will focus on the Options stage in the chapter about the GROW model (Chapter 7) and consider ways in which we can help the coachee to generate new ideas in three chapters about inspiring creativity (Chapters 11–13).

Selecting an option (15 minutes)

Once a number of options have been generated, the coachee should start to evaluate the relative merits of each possibility. She will be encouraged to select at least one option that she would like to pursue.

Committing to some actions (15 minutes)

In this part, the coach should encourage the coachee to commit to some actions that have emerged out of the coaching conversation, based on the option selected earlier. Some coachees like to develop an action plan that can be monitored.

Wrapping up, discussing how the coaching session went (10 minutes)

The final stage is a review of the coaching session, with an opportunity for the coachee to give the coach some feedback.

Relationship-related factors

In an important study about the success factors related to counselling interventions, Grencavage and Norcross (1990) detected four important elements. Firstly, they confirmed the importance of the relationship or 'working alliance' between the counsellor and the client. Secondly, they found that much of the success of these relationships depended on factors related to the client, such as her level of expectation and the nature and extent of pressure to make changes. Grencavage and Norcross found that the possibility of change (i.e. 'is the proposed change possible?') also played a significant role. It was recognised that any support available to the client (outside the counselling relationship) could have a significant impact on the outcome. This raises the following question: *What does the counsellor have most influence over?*

It seems to come down to a few very important factors. The way the counsellor interacts with her client is important. Grencavage and Norcross (1990) suggest that the warmth, attentiveness and positivity of the counsellor are important. Equally, the counsellor's 'ability to cultivate hope and positive expectancies within the client' is a significant factor (p. 374). In other words, the counsellor should behave and speak in a way which increases the client's optimism or hopefulness about the counselling intervention.

I would suggest that both of these factors apply to coaching as well. This means that coaches should adopt a warm, attentive and positive approach. We will discuss this further in Chapter 14, 'Being human'. A coach should also work to increase the positive expectations of the coachee (see Activity).

Level of confidence   Activity

Based on the research above, assuming that the two interventions are similar enough to make such claims, a coach should foster her coachee's confidence in the coaching process. This is much easier to achieve if the coach is confident about her own abilities.

(Continued)

(Continued)

Take a moment to reflect on your current levels of confidence about coaching. If you have started a learning journal, complete this activity on a new page. Otherwise, just find a blank sheet of paper.

At this moment, how confident are you about your ability to coach? Draw a line with a '0' on one end and a '10' on the other. On this scale, select a number that represents your current level of confidence. Below the line, write down some of your thoughts about why you selected that number. For example, if you have said '6', what makes it a '6' and not a '0'?

What practical things can you do in order to increase your self-rating? Make a note of a few things that you can do to increase your own assessment.

What makes the difference?

More recently, two leading executive coaches have suggested that the field of coaching has sometimes overlooked the many years of research that has gone into what makes psychotherapy successful (McKenna and Davis, 2009). According to their analysis of those studies, they conclude that there are some 'ingredients' that lead to successful outcomes in one-to-one relationships.

What accounts for the difference in outcomes between therapeutic relationships?

1. Client factors (40%)

Interestingly, the most significant difference between outcomes seemed to be based on factors outside the therapeutic relationship. The character of the client and what is happening in her life (her social network, her professional life, her family life) has a significant influence on the likelihood of a positive outcome.

2. The relationship (30%)

According to their analysis of the research into this area, 30% of the factors influencing the outcome of therapeutic relationships is the nature of the relationship between the therapist and her client. This means that the single most important factor *within the control of the therapist* is the strength and nature of the relationship.

3. Placebo or hope (15%)

Echoing the study by Grencavage and Norcross (1990) mentioned above, McKenna and Davis (2009) note that people on a waiting list for therapy start to improve even before the first session. Simply put, those that expect to benefit from therapy are more likely to do so. My own personal experience confirms that this happens in coaching too (see story from practice).

> In most of my executive coaching assignments, I contact the coachee prior to our first coaching session for an introductory conversation. I find out a bit more about the coachee and I say a few words about my own professional background. The conversation usually ends by discussing the broad topic that the coachee would like to explore at the first session. When we meet, I usually follow this up by asking how things are in relation to the topic that they mentioned on the phone. Very frequently, the coachee will report that things are actually better and that there have been improvements in the situation already.
>
> **Story from Practice**

Theory and techniques (15%)

According to McKenna and Davis (2009), hundreds of research papers over many years seem to point towards an uncomfortable reality. Despite the existence of many theories and approaches to psychotherapy, no one approach seems to be more effective than another. In the words of the authors of the study, 'It's not the particular model or tool that makes the difference. Nor is it the brilliant theoretical or experiential insights of the coach. It's how we engage the client to think and act on his own behalf' (p. 256). McKenna and Davis conclude by suggesting that a coach's belief in her approach is more important than the approach itself.

SNAPSHOT

INGREDIENTS:

Client factors (40%), Relationship (30%), Placebo (15%), Theory and techniques (15%)

Source: McKenna and Davis, 2009

Therapy is very different to coaching. However, they both depend on confidential, one-to-one relationships aimed at improving outcomes. Although the relative importance of each 'ingredient' may be different, it may be helpful to consider whether these factors are important in coaching relationships.

McKenna and Davis conclude by proposing some practical suggestions for coaches:

Firstly, 'use theory, models, tools, and techniques that you believe in and can deliver with competence and confidence' (p. 257).

Secondly, 'draw out and deepen the client's own theory of his situation and how he can deal with it most effectively'(p. 257). Rather than impose our theory and therefore a solution, it is important that the coachee understands her situation in a way that makes sense to her.

Thirdly, 'help the client to identify with precision the strengths she can bring to bear on the challenges ahead' (p. 257). In other words, you can support the coachee by helping her to highlight the strengths and resources that she already possesses.

Fourthly, 'be confident and clear about how the coaching process will work' (p. 257), highlighting the importance of a strong relationship between coach and coachee.

Finally, 'on a regular basis, ask the client whether she thinks you understand and appreciate her view of her situation' (p. 257). In other words, check that you have been able to show empathy.

McKenna and Davis's findings accord with some earlier work by Alexander and Renshaw (2005). According to them, in order for coaches to practice effectively, they should attend to three areas:

1. The relationship: Coaches must value their coachees, be open and honest in their interactions, and be able to support and challenge.
2. Being: Coaches must have self-confidence and be self aware.
3. Doing: The coach must be able to use effective processes and have a clear methodology. They need to have accomplished skills, being able to use both a clear framework and a range of effective coaching tools. (p. 381)

This book will cover all three areas, discussing the importance of the relationship in the 'Way of being' section (Chapters 14 and 15), coaching skills in the 'Key coaching skills' section (Chapters 3–6) a clear framework in the 'Coaching process' section (Chapters 7–9) and a range of effective coaching tools in the 'Practical tools and techniques' section (Chapters 10–13). The self-confidence and self-awareness will hopefully emerge as you read this book, undertake the exercises, watch the videos, practise coaching and reflect on your experiences.

We have considered some of the elements that lead to effective outcomes based on recent research. Before we move on to consider the skills related to coaching, I think it would be helpful to get a richer sense of what should be happening in a coaching conversation, and I would like to invite you to explore a metaphor which emerges from Whitmore's definition of coaching: 'unlocking people's potential to maximise their own performance' (2009: 11).

Unlocking potential: finding the key

Before we start considering the skills and process of coaching, let us briefly revisit Whitmore's definition of coaching so that we can be clearer about what you are working towards.

SNAPSHOT   Definition of coaching

'Unlocking people's potential to maximise their own performance.' (Whitmore, 2009: 11)

The notion of 'unlocking' in the English language implies the existence of a lock and therefore a 'key' that is needed to perform the act of 'unlocking'. This is a perfect metaphor for coaching and that is the reason that keys feature on the cover image of this book. This metaphor is particularly appealing and it may help us to explore the central essence of coaching.

Fundamental premise 1: Every coachee is able to achieve more than she is currently achieving

Firstly, if a person's potential is locked away, this suggests that it already exists within each person. That is one of the fundamental premises of coaching. Each person has almost unlimited potential, and certainly we, as coaches, must start from the belief that every coachee is able to achieve more than she is currently achieving. This positive belief is something that every coach must espouse. As we have seen in the discussion of ingredients, the hopefulness of the coachee has an impact on the success of a session. The coach's hopefulness and belief in the coachee play an important part in increasing and sustaining the hopefulness of the coachee.

Fundamental premise 2: The coachee must discover her own key

Secondly, the fact that coaching is about 'unlocking' potential means that the process of coaching is about finding a key that will allow the coachee to maximise her performance. So, we could say that the both coach and coachee are having a conversation in order to find that key. That is what the relationship is about. However, for coaching to be effective, the coachee must find the key for herself. The coach's role is to support the thinking and exploration of the coachee. Indeed, novice coaches often report that the most difficult task is resisting the urge to provide solutions. Using this analogy, the challenge arises when the coach thinks that she has discovered the 'key' and proudly hands it to the coachee saying 'there it is! Now you can use this to unlock your potential.' At best, this is patronising, at worst you can get in the way of the coachee discovering her own key. Less obvious but still unhelpful is the scenario in which the coach has seen the key and directs the coachee through leading questions and insinuation to find the key which the coach has already seen. Effective coaches will not look for the key themselves. Rather, they facilitate the coachee's search for the key. The most important moment in a coaching relationship is the one in which the *coachee* finds the key. This is often called the 'A-ha! moment' and will be discussed in Chapter 15 ('Inspiring others'). When the coachee discovers her own key, this gives her the positive emotion, the incentive and the self-belief to achieve more of her potential.

Activity   Discovering a key

Think back to a time when you discovered your own 'key' or solution to something. We often call these 'A-ha!' moments. We will revisit this concept later in this book. For now, write a paragraph or two in your learning journal about an 'A-ha!' moment that you have experienced. What was the situation, and how did you feel after the 'A-ha!' moment?

Story from Practice

I enjoy talking to students about coaching, and take every opportunity to do so. I was presenting an overview of coaching to a group of students on a Masters in Applied Positive Psychology (MAPP) programme at a university in London. As part of the exploration of the term 'coaching', I invited the students to get into groups to talk about the analogy of the key. This type of activity usually generates interesting insights into the nature of coaching relationships. On this occasion, students came up with some fantastic ideas that challenged my own thinking about this topic. One group was curious about whether it was OK for the coachee to believe that such a key did not exist. Another group wondered if some coaching conversations might be about the existence of multiple keys, with the coach supporting the coachee to identify the *right* key. Most interesting from my point of view was the idea that the coach and the coachee may sometimes be able to co-create the key needed to unlock the coachee's potential. These ideas are discussed briefly below.

Co-creating the key

Coaching is a partnership activity. In other words, both parties are involved in identifying ways forward. In this regard, it is possible to think of the alliance actually co-creating the key together. Through conversation, it is possible for the coach and the coachee to design a key that may unlock the coachee's potential. This is particularly helpful when the key has been 'lost'.

Too many keys?

In some coaching conversations, it may well be the case that the coachee is overwhelmed by opportunities or choices. She can see keys everywhere and cannot decide which, if any, to pick up. In these cases, the conversation can focus on which key might make the most difference, is best for the coachee at the moment or is the easiest to find and use.

No keys at all?

In other conversations, the coachee may feel that there is no key to unlock her potential. These conversations can be challenging, because of the centrality of the idea that coaching is about improving performance and enhancing well-being. In this case, it may be helpful to clarify the reason that the coachee has sought coaching. A good coaching conversation could focus around the topic of identifying goals for future sessions. To follow our analogy, the first coaching conversation could focus on a strategy for how to start looking for the key.

Conclusion

So after having considered some research and having explored the metaphor of the key, what can we conclude about 'becoming a coach? What are the attributes that we should develop if we are to be outstanding coaches who can make a real difference to others?

Being interested

To build effective relationships and encourage our coachees to talk and explore their thoughts and feelings, we must be able to show that we are genuinely interested in what they are saying. It is not that we must *look* interested, we must *be* interested in our coachees and what they are working through.

Being genuine

Coachees cannot build trusting relationships with people who are putting on a mask. Coaches must be genuine in their interactions. Lying, pretending and faking must be avoided. A coaching conversation should occur between two human beings who are honest and genuine.

Liking people

Some people make good money out of coaching. That said, the primary driver for every coach should be to support others to flourish. Coaches must like people. If this statement challenges you, that is OK. Coaching others will increase your appreciation of human beings. If you like people already, you simply have a significant head start!

Believing in people

Not only should a coach be a 'people person', she should also believe in others. We must give people the benefit of the doubt at all times. It is imperative that a coach believes that people are essentially good. Again, the practice of coaching can help to bolster this belief.

I hope that you are feeling energised and motivated about *becoming* a coach, even more than the idea of learning to coach. By this point, you should have a clearer idea about what coaching is and a better understanding of its purpose. We will now move on to the skills of coaching.

PART TWO

KEY COACHING SKILLS

3

LISTENING TO ENCOURAGE THINKING

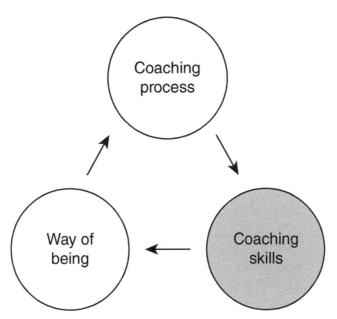

Figure 3.1 The three elements of effective coaching

In this chapter, we will consider the first of the coaching skills as we prepare to work through all three elements shown in Figure 3.1. This chapter is supported by some video clips of these skills being demonstrated during live coaching sessions. Some of you may wish to read about the skill first, and then watch the video. Others may find it useful to do this the other way round. Either will work!

Why listening is an important skill

Most of us use the skill of listening almost every day of our lives. What is different about listening for the purposes of coaching? Whereas we normally use our skills of conversational listening to understand what others are saying, in coaching, it is important to listen in a way that encourages the coachee to think more deeply and talk more openly. The ultimate aims of effective listening when coaching are that people enjoy speaking to the coach; that coachees are able to think *better*; and that coachees feel that they can be honest. Watch Video 3.2 which shows how the coachee can realise something about themselves just by talking.

FIND OUT MORE

This concept is best captured by Nancy Kline in *Time to Think* (1999). This book will provide you with an in-depth appreciation of the power of listening in coaching conversations.

Activity   Being listened to

Think back to a time when you were talking about something that was of genuine interest to you but the person you were speaking to was obviously distracted or not listening. How did that impact on what you were saying?

Often, poor quality listening can actually diminish the ability of the speaker to convey her message. If it seems to us that the person we are speaking to is uninterested, we can start to doubt the value of our topic. Fortunately, the opposite is also true. If people listen to us genuinely and attentively, we feel more confident about our topic and are able to think about and discuss it more fluently.

Story from Practice   When I deliver training on coaching skills, I like to run a short activity on the power of active listening. Participants are asked to work in pairs. One person in the pair is asked to think about a hobby or topic of interest and the other person is given a 'listening card'. The card instructs the participant to listen in a certain way. There are a range of different cards: 'active listening', 'attentive listening', 'less attentive listening' and 'not listening'. The 'active listening' card asks the participant to use her best listening skills, using positive affirmations, nodding and appropriate body language. The 'not listening' card instructs the participant to doodle on a piece of paper, interrupt the other person by asking seemingly irrelevant questions, jump in with her own experiences (e.g. 'that happened to me, too! In my case...') and look out of the window or otherwise seem distracted.

I dislike this activity because it can feel very disempowering and demotivating for the person who is partnered with someone with the 'not listening' card. The reason I still introduce this activity is because it can show so powerfully the difference between 'active listening' and 'not listening' on the person being listened to. Invariably, those who were listened to will feel positive and enthusiastic about their topic and will have enjoyed the chance to talk about it. On the other hand, those who experienced talking to someone with the 'not listening' card will have had a negative experience. Many participants report literally 'losing their voice' or feeling that their topic is 'boring' or 'silly'. The difference between the experiences is extreme. Coaching is all about active listening which makes a coachee feel as if she has been heard, that she is intelligent and that her topic is interesting. (Listening cards downloadable from SAGE Companion Website: **www.sagepub.co.uk/vannieuwerburgh**)

What can we do to improve the quality of our listening?

There are three key ways in which a person can enhance her listening skills: by learning some techniques that will demonstrate active listening; by learning about 'levels of listening'; and by becoming more curious. In this chapter, we will consider the techniques and levels of listening. Being curious will be explored in Chapter 14 ('Being human').

Techniques

At a superficial level, coaches need to ensure that they *look* like they are listening to their clients. These techniques may already be familiar to you and they are useful in many aspects of our lives. If you do these already, that is great – continue to do these things. If not, think about the value of adopting such techniques. As with any new skills, it will be necessary to practise these techniques. To coach effectively, it is not sufficient to *look* as if you are listening. You must actually be interested in what the coachee is saying.

Stay quiet

Stay quiet when people are talking to you about their experiences. For a variety of reasons, our society affords us little opportunity to be genuinely listened to. Often, a conversation is more like a battle for 'airtime'. It may be an exaggeration to say that we spend most of our time in conversations 'waiting for our turn to speak', but it can sometimes feel that way. If we start to plan how to respond to what the speaker is saying *while she is still talking*, this means that we have diverted some of our attention away from listening.

In coaching conversations, we must avoid the following:

a. Completing sentences

During coaching conversations, it is better to allow the coachee time to complete her own sentences. If the coachee is starting to think differently or see things from another perspective, it is normal that she will pause as she is talking, even in the middle of sentences. As coaches, we must control our (usually helpful) impulses to finish the sentences of our coachees. For example, a half-finished sentence such as 'I don't know ... there are times that this work gets so difficult, and there's just so little reward, I wonder whether to just...' can be completed in so many different ways. But there is a trap of attempting to demonstrate empathy by finishing such sentences for the coachee, e.g. 'retire early?' There are numerous reasons why this would be unhelpful. Firstly, it is often important for the coachee to struggle with the sentences for herself. If the idea of early retirement has been problematic in the past, the coachee saying it herself is very important so that she can experience what it feels like to say it out loud. Secondly, you will have necessarily made an assumption about what the coachee was going to say. There are dual risks here. We can offend the coachee by making a derogatory assumption (as in the example noted here, especially if the coachee did not consider herself to be of retirement age). On the other hand, the coachee may not feel able to contradict the coach, and therefore confusion is introduced. It can also be considered disrespectful to interrupt. Finally, we may be missing out on some insightful comments or realisations by the coachee.

b. Guessing at difficult words

Another temptation that may be perfectly acceptable in everyday conversation is providing suggestions for words that speakers seem to find difficult. This inclination is particularly unhelpful in coaching and should be avoided. To want to help a speaker to find exactly the right word is perfectly natural. But in coaching, the selection of words is critical. So we should encourage the coachee to come up with those words for herself. This applies even when the coachee asks 'what's the word?' or you are speaking to someone for whom English is an additional language. The choice of word, especially when it requires some hard thinking, is particularly important. As a coach, it is desirable to wait until the word has been selected. Usually it is worth unpicking why that particular word was selected, and this can often be quite interesting for the coachee. If the coach simply says, for example, 'the word you're looking for is "dichotomy"', many coaching opportunities are lost and the coachee may not feel fully listened to. Doing this also suggests impatience, when the coach should be demonstrating respect. The coachee should feel that she can have as much time as she wants to explore her topic. See how the coachee can recognise the importance of a specific word and how this significance can be explored by watching Videos 3.3 and 3.4.

c. Comparing ourselves

Again, this happens in normal conversations all the time. This is the 'it happened to me' scenario. In a two-way conversation, this is good as it keeps the conversation moving between both parties. In coaching, it is less welcome because it takes the focus of the discussion off the coachee and onto the coach. The purpose of the coaching session is to give the coachee thinking and speaking time. For example, if a coachee says 'it was three weeks before I met my line manager', it might be very tempting for her coach to reply with 'Yes, I know how that works. It was the same for me. Mind you, I wasn't too bothered...' etc. This may seem to be a good way of demonstrating empathy, but what in fact happens is that the conversation turns to focus on you, as a coach, instead of the coachee, where the focus must remain at all times. When you are being coached, take advantage of this situation! When you are the coach, note any thoughts like this but do not compare yourself. If it is necessary or helpful to inform the coachee that you have been in a similar situation, keep it very brief. Using the example above, 'I had a similar experience. How did that make you feel?' is sufficient. In other words, share the fact that you have had a similar experience *if you think that this information will be helpful for the coachee,* and then turn the focus back on the coachee's experience of the situation.

d. One-upmanship

This is probably unhelpful in any conversation. This refers to comments that are intended to show that you are better or that you have had an even more amazing experience than the speaker. Referring back to the example above: 'Three weeks? I don't think I met my manager for well over a year!' Such comments minimise the experience of the other person, and therefore have no place in a coaching conversation.

e. Doodling

While some people would argue that they are able to listen better when they doodle, this is not conducive to good listening in coaching conversations. This allows us to consider a very important point of principle when it comes to coaching. As important as listening attentively to the coachee is the need to *demonstrate* that you are listening. Both must be happening. So, even if a coach may feel that she *does* listen better when she doodles, the issue is that it may not be perceived in that way by the coachee.

> At one point in my professional life, I had a manager who used to ask me to talk to her while she was typing emails: 'Talk to me. I can listen to you while I respond to this email.' Even if she did have this amazing ability to type and listen at the same time, my perception that she was not focusing on what I had to say meant that I was less able to express myself.
>
> **Story from Practice**

f. Looking at other things

As we will discuss later, the use of eye contact is very important in coaching. Therefore, looking over the coachee's shoulder to see what is going on in the corridor, or noticing an unusual aircraft through the window is unhelpful. However discreetly you do this, it is very likely that the coachee will notice. Avoid being distracted by other visual cues – noticing something outside the window, inspecting your fingernails, looking with interest at a piece of furniture – all these things will get in the way of good listening.

> **Story from Practice**
>
> As a coach, I tend to sit in a way that means that I am facing the wall to minimise visual distractions. Coachees are less easily distracted, especially as they should be busy thinking and talking for most of the coaching session. If they are engaged and interested in what they are talking about, they will not notice people outside (even if the room has a glass wall).
>
> In order to keep an eye on time, I place my watch or mobile phone between us somewhere very obvious, so that there is no need to glance in other directions. Another way of doing this is to look at the coachee's watch, although you will need to develop your ability to read the time upside down!

g. Fidget

Become aware of any unintentional fidgeting that you may do. The best way of discovering these is to film yourself coaching. Most people do not really know what it looks like when they are coaching. Small behaviours, such as drumming fingers, clicking pens and twiddling thumbs, can be distracting, and may also suggest to the coachee that the coach is bored or impatient.

Activity   Try going to your local coffee shop on your own. While enjoying your drink, observe others. Who is actively listening? How can you tell? Can you notice mirroring of body language? In other words, are both people leaning towards each other? Is one person obviously listening to the other? What can you tell about the relationship just by noticing body language? Make notes in your learning journal.

So, for coaching, there should be a different dynamic from everyday conversations. It should not have a back-and-forth feel. Rather, it is more like one person talking and the other person listening. Coaches recommend a ratio of 20/80 or even 10/90 of the coach speaking. So it is natural for this to feel unfamiliar at first because social conversations tend to work best at 50/50 or 40/60. Take a few moments to watch Video 3.5 'Coach listening actively, coachee allowed to think' and Video 3.6 'Coach uses silence to encourage coachee to create a strategy'.

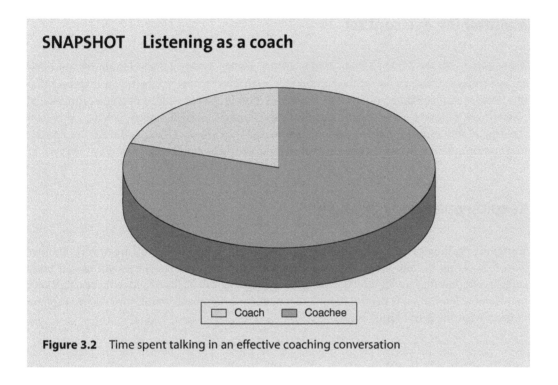

SNAPSHOT   Listening as a coach

Coach   Coachee

Figure 3.2 Time spent talking in an effective coaching conversation

Twenty words   Activity

Practise limiting the amount of time you speak. Challenge yourself by allocating yourself only 20 words in a conversational interaction. If you only allow yourself 20 words in a conversation, you'll have to be very careful about how you use them! Note your reflections after doing this exercise in your learning journal.

Purposeful listening

When coaching, we listen with a different purpose. We want to allow the coachee an opportunity to speak, or to have a voice. Coaches must focus on listening *for meaning*. The purpose is to respectfully understand the situation or experience of the coachee. Being respectful entails being interested and open to a person's experiences. Especially important is the idea of not 'knowing' the other person's experiences or 'what it's like'. Understanding the situation is not the coach's primary purpose. As discussed above, the primary purpose is to enhance the coachee's ability to think well and deeply about the topic that she has brought to a coaching session.

Maintaining eye contact

It is important to show a keen interest in what the coachee is saying by maintaining appropriate eye contact. Once you start to intentionally manage your eye contact, you may find that this is more complex than you initially imagined. This is because different cultures and social classes have different expectations regarding eye contact. Coaches need to have an understanding of different cultural norms and ensure that they are providing sufficient eye contact to communicate respect and interest in what their coachees are saying.

Keeping open body language

Your body position can also give out subtle messages about how open you are to what another person is saying to you. Coachees may start the early coaching sessions with closed body language, as they may be slightly defensive. Body language will be discussed in more detail later in this book. For now, it is helpful to note that open body language invites the coachee to share more of what she is thinking.

What About You?

How do you sit when you are most comfortable? Even if you are comfortable in that position, how might others interpret it?

Matching and mismatching level of energy

Coaches need to manage their levels of energy in relation to the coachee. For example, if a coachee is very excitable and drawn in many directions, it may be helpful for the coach to be less excited, perhaps showing more calmness. On the other hand, if the coachee is very sedate and quiet when trying to generate new ideas, it may be helpful for the coach to be a bit more energetic. Usually, in the first part of the coaching conversation, it is helpful to match the coachee's level of energy because it is a good way of building rapport. In the latter part of the coaching conversation, the coach may sometimes try to counterbalance the coachee's level of energy. How loudly a coachee speaks may give an indication of her levels of energy. This also applies to the coach. Watch Video 3.7 to see how the coach can match the coachee's level of energy by laughing together.

What About You?

How loudly do you speak in most situations? If you consistently speak loudly or very softly, be aware of the implications of this in a coaching session. A very softly spoken coach will bring a sense of calmness and relaxation to a coaching session. A coach who is boisterous will bring excitement and energy. A good coach needs to be able to vary this based on the best interests of the coachee. It is a good idea to aim to end the coaching conversation on a positive, up-beat and high energy note.

Seating arrangement

This may seem like a detail but the arrangement and choice of seating play an important role. How people sit during a coaching conversation can influence how the conversation progresses. Ideally, there should be no physical obstacles between coach and coachee. But it is also important to ensure that each person has enough 'personal space' for themselves. As a matter of principle, coaches and coachees should consider themselves to be equal. For this reason, coach and coachee should be sitting on the same type of chair. When one person sits on a grand leather office chair and the other person is sitting on a plastic stool, there can be no equality. If you would like to introduce any activities, it may be helpful to have a table nearby.

Encouraging nods and sounds

Encouraging noises and words like 'uh-huh', 'go on', 'oh, I see' show the coachee that you are listening and interested in what she has to say. When used in the natural gaps in a person's speech, it can also reinforce the fact that you will not be interrupting – allowing the other person to take her time explaining something or exploring an idea. Watch Video 3.8 to see how you might listen to the coachee in an encouraging and non-judgemental way.

HOW TO MANAGE SILENCES

Silences are a key feature of good coaching conversations. Often, silences precede important realisations by the coachee (and the coach). This will be discussed later in Chapter 15 ('Inspiring others'). However, this can be at odds with social norms. Social etiquette in many cultures suggests that it is polite to keep conversations going by filling silences. A gap in a conversation can seem awkward and uncomfortable, and without knowing it, many of us have techniques and strategies for filling these silences.

In coaching, silences are desirable. Firstly, they can create 'thinking time' for the coachee. Secondly, allowing a coachee time to reflect quietly without interruption can demonstrate respect. Finally, silences encourage a deeper and more meaningful conversation. So silences can build serenity into a conversation. It can also demonstrate your respect for the other person by showing that 'silences are OK'. It is a very positive way of demonstrating unconditional positive regard. You are, in effect, saying that you will view the coachee positively whether or not she has anything to say. Video 3.9 shows a good example of how silence can be used to encourage the coachee to take responsibility.

FIRST STEP: Notice when silences occur

Normally, our alarm system kicks in. In normal, day-to-day situations, silences are perceived as 'awkward' or 'uncomfortable'. (The only exception seems to be when we are in elevators when such silences are expected!) So many of us are socially conditioned to be alert for potential silences in conversations. In the first instance, do your best to notice when these silences occur, accepting that they may be a normal part of a coaching conversation.

SECOND STEP: Do not implement the emergency procedure

Once a silence descends, it is tempting for a novice coach to blurt out a follow-up question to relieve the perceived tension. However, silence following a question may indicate that the coachee has been encouraged to think carefully. Remember, we are listening to encourage new thinking. So, in a sense, silence following a question is likely to be an indication that you have asked a very good, thought-provoking question. Stated differently, if the coachee is able to answer a question immediately, this may suggest that she did not need to think or contemplate anything new before answering.

We will discuss the skill of 'asking powerful questions' in the next chapter. Sometimes a coachee's question can pose a dilemma for the coach. Coachees often ask 'do you know what I mean?' or 'can you see where I'm coming from?' When a coach is actively listening to a coachee, this question can be challenging to answer. On the one hand, we know that it is important to build rapport with the coachee. From that point of view, it would make sense to say 'Yes, I know *exactly* what you mean.' However, although most of us would feel encouraged by such a response, it also negates the need for the coachee to explain further. Our main intention is to get the coachee to speak as much as possible.

In my own experience, clients have often realised something significant only when they have spoken it out. For example, one client said 'I didn't realise why I was so annoyed about this relationship until just now.' So, on the one hand it is important for us to maintain rapport, but also important not to assume that we 'get' what the client is saying before they've described the situation fully.

Story from Practice

It is tricky if the coachee asks 'Do you know what I mean?' or a similar question. Below are a few answers that I have given:

- 'What you've said so far makes sense. Please carry on.'
- 'I think I'm getting a picture of what it's like. Tell me more.'
- 'It's becoming clearer…' [followed by a brief summary of what the coachee has said so far]

Here is an example conversation:

Coachee: I don't know if I've explained that very well…
Coach: Take your time.
Coachee: I'm not making any sense, am I?
Coach: I think it's worth exploring.
Coachee: I can't explain how I feel about this.
Coach: Could you try?
Coachee: It feels like a muddle. I'm in a maze. Do you know what I mean?
Coach: It's becoming a bit clearer. So, it feels like a muddle to you?
Coachee: Yes, that's the right word. It's a bit of a muddle. On the one hand, I feel that I should be grateful for the opportunity. But on the other, I feel that this work should be recognised by the organisation. That's probably the real issue.

In all cases, silences from the coach will show that it is OK for the coachee not to be able to articulate what she is thinking straight away. We are aiming for increased self-awareness and perhaps the ability of the coachee to see her situation from a different perspective.

Levels of listening

In an influential book about coaching and mentoring, Hawkins and Smith (2006) identify four levels of listening which are helpful to consider here.

1. 'Attending'

At this level, the coach would give the coachee her 'full and undivided' attention (p. 213). This includes focusing on the coachee and giving the appropriate non-verbal signals that the coach is interested in what the coachee has to say.

2. 'Accurate listening'

To listen accurately, the coach must not only be fully attentive but also be able to reflect back the content of what the coachee has said, either directly or by paraphrasing. Matching the language or sensory modes used (e.g. 'I feel' or 'I see') can demonstrate accurate listening to the coachee.

3. 'Empathic listening'

This type of listening builds on the previous two levels. According to Hawkins and Smith, 'this involves listening not only to the words being spoken, but also to the feelings being conveyed' (p. 213). Listening in this way means that the coach is able to acknowledge the feelings of the coachee and reflect these back to her.

4. 'Generative empathic listening'

This is the highest level of listening identified by Hawkins and Smith. At this level, the coach is 'able to play back the thoughts and feelings that are on the periphery' of the coachee's awareness (p. 214). In some cases, the coach can pick up a sense, a feeling or thought that the coachee may not be fully aware of herself.

What About You?

Take a moment to reflect on how you are listened to on most days. What level of listening is most common in your everyday life? When are you listened to at level 3 or level 4? What does it feel like when you are listened to in that way?

When you are listening to others, what is the level of listening that you do most often? Are there certain situations when level 1 listening is helpful? Write a few lines in your learning journal about how you currently listen to others.

To be an effective coach, it is necessary to be able to work at the first three levels identified by Hawkins and Smith (2006). Level 1 listening (being fully attentive) and level 2 listening (hearing what the coachee has said and being able to reflect this back accurately) are essential for every coaching session. At these levels, the coachee will feel that you have listened to her and that you have been able to understand what she has said. Often level 3 listening (empathic listening) can be a powerful experience for the coachee. Not only has the coach been attentive, and heard what the coachee has said but she has also picked up the emotions and non-verbal communications of the coachee. As novice coaches, developing and practising level 3 listening is an important part of your development.

Level 4 listening is a more challenging concept. This requires much more intuition and can be risky. At level 4, the coach is able to sense feelings and thoughts that are just on the edge of a person's awareness. Coaches who are able to listen at this level report that they get a 'gut feeling' or a 'sense' that there is something that is not being said. For experienced coaches, it is sometimes worth the risk of sharing this feeling or sense with the coachee to see whether this resonates with her. However, this level of listening is not essential for effective coaching, and it is not recommended for novice coaches.

We have considered some techniques and different levels of listening. Hopefully, you now have an enhanced appreciation of the importance of listening to encourage thinking. Practice is the best way of developing this skill. We will now proceed to a closely related skill: asking powerful questions.

4

ASKING POWERFUL QUESTIONS

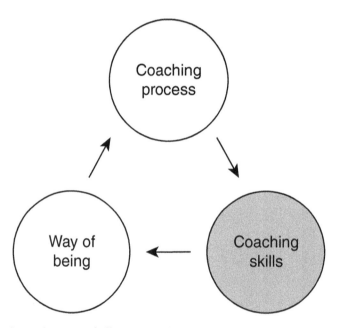

Figure 4.1 The three elements of effective coaching

Asking questions is one of the key skills of coaching. And yet, like listening, one could argue that this is also a basic skill of conversation. This chapter considers the skill of asking powerful (thought-provoking) questions for the purposes of coaching. As you will see below, the use of questions in coaching may be different from their use in our everyday lives. In coaching, questions can be used in a multiplicity of ways. They can be used to clarify, provoke new thoughts, challenge and elicit information. That makes it important for the coach to be able to determine what type of question will be most helpful in different situations. When we consider the GROW coaching process (Chapter 7), I will propose that some types of questions are more appropriate at certain stages of the framework.

Types of question

There are four types of questions of interest to coaches: closed, open, leading and multiple questions.

Closed question: A closed question is one that can be answered with a single word (e.g. 'yes' or 'no') or a short phrase. Generally speaking, they are straightforward to answer and can provide the questioner with specific information, facts and numerical data. For example, 'How often do you exercise in a week?' or 'Can you speak French?' are closed questions.

Open question: An open question is the opposite of a closed question. It intentionally invites longer, more thoughtful answers. For example, 'How would you describe your attitude to work?' or 'What encouraged you to become a coach?' are open questions. If we reflect back to the 20/80 balance of listening (coaches should be listening for about 80% of the time and coachees should be listening for about 20% of the time), it becomes apparent that open questions are an integral part of coaching conversations.

The 'Yes–No' game   Activity

Find someone (playful) to practise with. This should be enjoyed as a game and can be played at home, in the car or at work.

One person takes the role of 'Questioner' and it is her role to ask open questions. The other person, 'Speaker', chooses a topic that is of interest to her (e.g. Vietnamese food). The Questioner's intention is to ask as many open questions in a row as possible. After every question, the Speaker should be given ample opportunity to answer. The Speaker's intention is to catch the Questioner asking a closed question, so will be attempting to answer 'Yes' or 'No' at any opportunity provided. The Questioner wins if the conversation lasts for 5 minutes without being caught out. The Speaker wins if they can legitimately answer 'Yes' or 'No' to any question asked. This includes sub-questions such as 'isn't it?' Give it a go. It's more difficult than it sounds!

Increasing the use of open questions   Activity

Without telling others what you are doing, simply try increasing the proportion of open questions that you ask (at work or at home). Observe the change in dynamic of your conversations. When you have tried this, make notes in your learning journal about how it changes the dynamic of the conversation.

Leading question: A leading question is one that manipulates the listener to think in a particular way. Some leading questions actually contain the preferred answer within them. For example, 'Would it be helpful if you spoke to your colleagues about the proposed changes?' is a leading question. Although framed as a question, there is a clear suggestion ('speak to your colleagues about the proposed changes') embedded in the sentence. Leading questions are manipulative and should not be used in coaching. While giving advice is not recommended, it is preferable to using leading questions to direct a coachee to a presumed solution.

Multiple questions: These are a series of questions posed one after the other without an opportunity for the listener to attempt an answer. For example: 'What is the best way of managing such a complex team? I mean, is it better to simply tell them what to do? And anyway, what is the point of consulting with people when the decision has already been made?' are a series of multiple questions. While acceptable in everyday conversations, they can be particularly unhelpful in coaching. A series of questions in quick succession can disorient the coachee. In addition, it is likely that the coachee will only answer the last question, ignoring or forgetting the earlier ones.

Using questions with intent

So to return to the idea of *intention*, closed questions are ideal if the coach is trying to clarify some aspect of what the coachee has said ('Do you work in the same office as your manager?'), ascertain numerical data ('How many people are in your marketing team?) or extract a clear 'yes' or 'no' answer ('So you're *disappointed* with the latest statistics?'). Closed questions are also easier for the coachee to answer, so can be used at the beginning of the conversation to get it started ('Are you based in London?'; 'Do you commute to work?'; 'Would you like a cup of coffee?').

On the other hand, if the intention is to provide the coachee with an opportunity to think through a particular situation, open questions may be more helpful. Bearing in mind the 80/20 or 90/10 balance of listening to speaking mentioned in the previous chapter, closed questions would be very unhelpful. Almost by definition, the closed question takes longer to ask than for the listener to answer.

Good open questions start with 'how' or 'what'. For example, 'What are the main reasons for your change of heart?' or 'How would you go about reclaiming your authority?' Fulfilling the same function as an open question is any statement that invites the coachee to speak: 'Tell me more about...' or 'Please describe how...' 'I'd love to hear your thoughts about...'

SNAPSHOT   Thought-provoking questions and statements

How could you...
How would you describe...
How might this situation...

What would you...
What other options...
What makes this situation...
Tell me more about...
Please describe...
I would like to hear your perspective on...

Leading questions are possibly the most challenging traps for novice coaches. It seems that it is now commonly accepted that one of the best ways of helping someone is to give her advice about what to do. As a result, it seems to happen very frequently, meaning that most people are very good at giving advice. What is positive about the situation is that there is a good intention behind advice-giving: to help others. Coaching expert Jim Knight addresses this challenge when he writes about the 'complexity of helping' (2011): 'To bring about the improvements we hope to see, we need to recognize – in fact, honor – the complexity of providing support within professional relationships' (p. 20). Knight proposes that there are five factors that should be considered by coaches.

1. Change: Many people are unaware of the need to change or improve. They cannot see how others perceive them.
2. Status: Coaches must ensure that they do not present themselves as being of higher status than their coachees. According to Knight, 'Skilful coaches use a variety of subtle communication strategies to create equality' between themselves and their coachees (p. 22).
3. Identity: The way we see ourselves, our identity, is often connected to our professional roles. 'Our understanding of how good and competent we are is frequently tied to our success or failure in our work' (p. 23). Coaches need to be sensitive to this.
4. Thinking: It is important that the person we are coaching is involved in the thinking process. Most often, people do not want others to do the thinking for them. The coachee must feel that she is the lead thinker in the relationship.
5. Motivation: What the coachee is working on must matter to her. If the topic does not matter to the coachee, there is little incentive for her to make any changes.

Notice your tendency to give advice   Activity

As you start to coach others, be aware of your tendency to give advice or provide sugges-tions. It is very normal for novice coaches to fall into these traps in the early stages. During coaching sessions, simply make a mental note every time you find yourself giving advice. When the session is over, reflect on how often this happened, and what motivated you to provide the advice. Take notes in your learning journal, reflecting on the reasons that you felt compelled to provide advice. Also jot down some ideas about how to manage similar situations in future.

Perhaps the real paradox is that most of us are better at giving advice than being gracious about taking advice! In any case, coaching is about allowing others to find their own ways forward – not telling people what to do or pointing out the 'obvious' solutions. Hopefully, the analogy of the key we considered in Chapter 2 was helpful in this regard. The power of coaching comes from the fact that the coach supports the coachee to find the key for herself. The experience of discovering the key is what can inspire and motivate the coachee, building her self-esteem and confidence.

As novice coaches become aware of a tendency to give advice or provide solutions, they will start to withhold such comments. However, the intention to solve the coachee's problem can sometimes be apparent when a coach replaces the advice or suggestion with a leading question. For example, if the coach thinks that the coachee should not respond to work-related emails over the weekend, she may ask a question similar to this one: 'Is there any way of switching your smart phone off over the weekend?' It looks like a simple closed question. But is there more to it?

While acceptable in everyday conversations, multiple questions can be counterproductive in coaching. Generally speaking, multiple questions seem to be more likely when the coach or coachee is in an excited or anxious state, or when a conversation is rushed. They occur most often when the coach attempts to 'correct' a question which she has just asked, providing a second, 'better' question. Even if, as the coach, you feel that you have thought of a more incisive question, it is good practice to allow the coachee to answer your initial query. Coachees can be trusted to let you know if your question is obscure or difficult to answer. That can be your cue for rewording the question, if necessary.

Activity   Improve the quality of your coaching questions

First task: Notice advice-giving

Notice when you have given advice or provided a solution to the coachee.
Reflect on your intention. What was driving you to give advice or provide a solution? What can you do the next time that you are tempted to give advice?

Second task: Notice when you've withheld advice

Be alert for situations in which you have wanted to give advice but managed to withhold it. How did it feel to withhold advice? What was the outcome?

Third task: Make a note of any leading questions

Reflect on your questions. Were there any leading questions? How did you manage this?

Fourth task: Check for multiple questions

Note any occasions when you ask a second question before the coachee has answered the first. What was the reason for the second question? What made you want to ask it before the coachee had answered the first? What strategies can you use to minimise the chances of this happening in future?

Beyond asking questions to get answers

Apart from the functional aspects of questions that we have discussed above, they play an important role in building relationships between coach and coachee. Questions can be pivotal in creating the right environment for effective coaching conversations. Used intentionally, questions *demonstrate* curiosity which is a necessary 'way of being' for a coach (this is discussed further in Chapters 14 and 15). By asking questions, the coach shows that she is interested in the coachee and her topic. Showing an interest in someone else is often the best way of building meaningful relationships.

Perhaps even more importantly, certain types of questions can create thoughtful and reflective environments. For example, 'And what is it about this situation that makes you feel uneasy?' is likely to lead to a meaningful response. The question 'So what is your level of motivation in relation to this change programme?' is much more likely to encourage reflection than 'What's your view about this change programme?' It is difficult to answer well-crafted questions without giving them some thought. Thought-provoking questions do not have to be 'clever' questions. In fact, most often they are relatively short. For example 'What made you do that?' or 'And how did that make you feel?' can be thought-provoking questions. There are two obvious ways to find out if your questions are thought-provoking. First, a silence from the coachee before she answers the question is a good sign. (That is why we must be able to manage silences. Those silences represent the time that the coachee is starting to engage in new thinking.) Secondly, ask the coachee about the quality of your questions. Any responses suggesting that the questions 'made me think' can be considered a strong endorsement of your coaching practice.

Take a few moments to watch Video 4.2 'Coach challenges coachee with a thought-provoking question' and Video 4.3 'Coach asks a thought-provoking question'.

This is one of the real strengths of coaching: it creates environments for quality thinking. Coaches need to ask thought-provoking questions so that coachees get into a more reflective mode than when they are busy doing what they always do. For example, in most social situations, the question 'How are you?' is not meant as a genuine invitation for a full answer. It is expected that others will say something bland such as 'fine' or 'not too bad'. It may be the case that social interactions actually minimise the possibility for meaningful conversations. On the other hand, if you can create reflective spaces that encourage meaningful conversations, asking 'How are you today?' to a coachee may elicit a much more thoughtful response. The key difference is that coaches demonstrate that they have a genuine interest in the answer.

In addition, powerful questions can inspire creativity and new thinking. One of the roles of a coach is to support the coachee to see things differently. For example, a question like 'If all of your management team resigned tomorrow, and you were given full control of the strategic direction of this organisation, what would you propose?' might help a coachee to see things from a different angle. The thought-provoking question 'If you knew that you could not fail, what would you do in this situation?' can unlock creative ideas.

> **Story from Practice**
>
> Having heard the phrase 'If I were king for a day'* at a conference in the US, I asked this question during a coaching conversation: 'If you were king for a day, how would you change what's happening in your organisation at the moment?' Having grappled with the issue of 'lack of communication' within the coachee's department for two coaching sessions with limited success, this question allowed the coachee to see the situation completely differently. 'If I were king for a day, I would decree that everyone should share important information with others, when they think it's relevant for others.' I asked how that decree could be implemented, wondering 'what would have to happen within the organisation?' In discussing how the king's decree would be implemented, the coachee realised that the issue of 'relevance' was more complicated than he had originally thought. 'I guess that it is going to be a balance of sharing the information with the right people', he said. Finally, he concluded that there should be a mix of ways in which interested people could access information. For key stakeholders, the information would be sent in a variety of formats. However, this information would not be sent to everyone. Others who were not directly involved in the project would be given the opportunity to join an email list. Finally, all the correspondence would be posted online for anyone who was interested in finding out more. Being king for 20 minutes allowed the coachee to see the situation from a completely different perspective, and this led to a helpful insight for the coachee. And this was triggered by one thought-provoking question.
>
> ―――――――――――
>
> *With thanks to Bob Marzano.

Questions can also be used to seek commitment. Often, closed questions can be helpful here: 'Are you confident that you will be able to follow through with this?' or 'What is the percentage chance of success if you do what you've just suggested?' Video 4.4 shows a coach seeking commitment to action from the coachee.

So asking *thought-provoking* questions is a key skill for you to develop. As coaches, we need to move away from questions that help *us* to understand a situation or provide a solution. This can be a liberating experience, allowing us to focus more intently on helping the coachee to increase her own awareness of the situation. Bob Thomson provides a thought-provoking challenge when he suggests that we should ask questions 'with no attachment to the answer' (2012). In other words, as coaches, we should not be asking particular questions *in order* to get to specific outcomes or answers we have an interest in.

Using questions to elicit precision

It can be helpful, at times, to invite the coachee to be more precise in her descriptions. This can help to uncover any assumptions or significance in what has been shared. For example,

'People don't seem to appreciate it when I share my personal opinion' could be challenged with the following question: 'When you say 'people', who are you referring to?' See how you can ask a question to elicit precision by watching Video 4.5.

> ## SNAPSHOT   Examples of questions to elicit precision
>
> Coachee: 'I used to enjoy my work, but now I don't.'
> Coach: 'There is nothing you enjoy in relation to your work?'
>
> Coachee: 'I guess there are some things that I might have done differently.'
> Coach: 'What kind of things?'
>
> Coachee: 'People don't like it when I'm very honest about what I think.'
> Coach: 'Who are you referring to?'

Using questions to manage the conversation

Questions can also be used to move a conversation along by focusing on a future state ('So how will doing this help you achieve your goal?') or by bringing the coachee back to the original topic ('How does this relate to your original topic?'). As we study the GROW coaching process (in Chapter 7), you will see how questions can be used to move coachees from one stage to the next.

Asking questions without knowing the answers

As coaches we may need to build up our courage to ask questions that neither we nor our coachees have answers to. The fact that there is no simple answer necessitates new thinking. This can be unsettling at first, especially if the coachee looks to the coach for an answer. However, the shared sense of 'not knowing' and working together to find an answer lies at the very heart of coaching practice.

Questions and the way they are used in some of our educational systems create a strange situation where coachees may think that the coach must know the answer before asking the question. The same line of thinking assumes that there might be one, 'right', answer, and that the coach is waiting for the coachee to provide it. Therefore, it is important for the coach to create a climate that is more open and exploratory (see Snapshot below).

SNAPSHOT   How to create open and exploratory learning spaces

1. Demonstrate that you do not necessarily know the answer to a question that you have asked. This can be done very explicitly by saying, 'I don't know the answer to this question, but...'
2. Demonstrate that there is no 'right' answer to your questions. This can be done by being non-judgemental about a coachee's answers, accepting each as a possible and equally valued response. Asking 'How many different ways could you answer that question?' will also make the point that there are many possible responses.
3. Ensure that the coachee's answers are based on what she thinks, rather than what she thinks the coach wants to hear. An indication that a coachee is providing an answer that meets the approval of the coach is that the statement ends with an implied question mark.

Coach: 'How else could you improve your chances at interview?'
Coachee: 'I guess I should probably spend more time planning for it?'

or

Coach: 'What opportunities does this situation present to you?'
Coachee: 'A chance to apply for the manager's job?'

In both examples, the coachee is seeking approval from the coach. It is helpful to explicitly reject the invitation to become an adviser by asking 'What do you think? Does that sound like a good option to you?' Video 4.6 shows you a good example of this.

What About You?

Think of the most recent time that you asked a question that you did not know the answer to. What was the context? Are there situations in which you would avoid asking questions that you did not know the answer to?

Favourite questions

As we consider the GROW process later in this book (Chapter 7), you are invited to collect 'favourite' questions for the various stages. As a coach, you will start to create your own questions which are consistently helpful at the different stages. Some coaches have a selection of 'favourite questions'. Most often, however, the most helpful question will emerge from a coachee's response if the coach is listening genuinely.

What About You?

What one thing can you do from now on to greatly increase the effectiveness of the questions that you ask?

Broadening your array of questions will improve your coaching practice. It will also be helpful in many other situations, including the questions you ask yourself. The craft of asking thought-provoking questions is, however, only part of what is required. Coaches must also be curious. It seems that we are born with an insatiable curiosity. You only need to watch one- or two-year old babies to notice that they are naturally inquisitive. As coaches, we must find a way to tap into that natural (and sometimes latent) sense of curiosity.

If we are able to attend fully to the coachee and demonstrate that we understand what she is saying (as discussed in Chapter 3), and bring with us a natural sense of curiosity about the coachee and her situation, this will greatly enhance the likelihood of a positive outcome for the coachee. Curiosity will provide us, as coaches, with appropriate questions and prevent us from falling into the trap of finding solutions for our coachees.

Being curious   Activity

As with all the other activities in this book, it is up to you whether you undertake this. However, this is a particularly important activity, so please consider ways of finding the necessary time.

Although we are born inquisitive, the level of our curiosity can decrease over time. Perhaps as we have more experiences, we learn more and therefore feel that we have less to be curious about. However, for coaching, it is important to rekindle this spirit of curiosity which will enhance our presence, our listening and our questioning.

For this activity, you should identify an experience in which your natural curiosity will be aroused. Find some time just for yourself (between one hour and one weekend) when you can indulge yourself by going somewhere to find out more about something you are interested in, but know very little about. This could be a visit to a motor museum, an aquarium, the zoo, a cathedral, a small village you have heard about, a sporting event, an underground bunker or anything that sparks your imagination. The indulgence relates to the time that you invest in the activity. If, for example, you have always been interested in capuchin monkeys, allow yourself a

(Continued)

(Continued)

couple of hours at the zoo, just watching them. If there's a town or village that you have never been to, but is of interest to you, perhaps spend the whole afternoon, walking around. If you've always wanted to ride a motorcycle, fly a plane, learn to ski, spend some time in a place that will give you more information about the activity. The purpose of this activity is to allow yourself time to be curious. That is all. You need to be interested and you need to make sure that you are there for no other purpose than 'finding out'. Take your learning journal with you, and simply write down every question that comes to your mind during your experience. When you have concluded your experience, write down your thoughts about how it felt.

Hopefully, you have not skipped over the activity above. At the very least, I hope that you have scheduled some time to pursue an activity that will unlock your natural curiosity. Let us now move to the third set of coaching-related skills: summarising and paraphrasing.

5

PARAPHRASING AND SUMMARISING

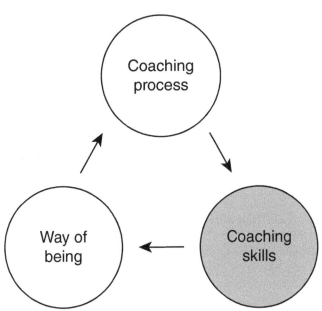

Figure 5.1 The three elements of effective coaching

Paraphrasing and summarising are two related skills required by coaches. By emphasising the abilities of listening and asking questions, summarising and paraphrasing can sometimes be undervalued. They are just as vital to a good coaching conversation. This chapter will explain why they are an essential part of a coach's skill set.

It is fair to wonder whether there is any real difference between 'summarising' and 'paraphrasing'. Often the words are used interchangeably and are sometimes considered to be synonyms. When used for the purposes of academic writing, there is a clear distinction. The word 'paraphrasing' refers to the act of presenting existing written information using a different form of words. When you paraphrase, you are conveying the same meaning using your own choice of words. Usually the purpose is to elucidate meaning. It is a way of checking understanding. As a result, both the original piece of writing and the new version will have roughly the same number of words. Summarising is different. In the same context, 'summarising' is used by a writer to convey a message which is based on the original text but using fewer words. The summary is a shorter version of the original. Some sources even suggest how much shorter a summary should be than the original. When we talk about academic writing, the distinction seems obvious but not particularly significant. When used in coaching there is an important difference. Each should be used intentionally and with a clear purpose.

Paraphrasing in coaching

When coaching, paraphrasing refers to the act of reflecting back what the coachee has said. The intention is not to provide a brief account, but to present information back to the coachee in order to check the meaning of what has just been said. One reason we do this is to raise the awareness of the coachee. The other is to confirm that both the coach and the coachee are talking about the same thing. In coaching, as in academic writing, paraphrasing is not about saying something with fewer words. Paraphrasing is particularly helpful when the coachee is exploring her understanding of a situation or coming to terms with a dilemma. Video 5.2 offers a good example of paraphrasing in practice.

SNAPSHOT   Paraphrasing when coaching

Coachee: 'I don't know... Sometimes it feels like people want me to be more decisive but when I do make a decision, nobody is prepared to support me personally.'

Coach: 'It sounds like you're not certain about what people want. It feels to you like others want you to be more decisive, but when you behave that way, you don't get any support.'

Sometimes, hearing back what was said, in the voice of another person, can provide a new perspective or insight for the coachee. There have been many times, in my own practice as a coach, when I have repeated, almost word for word, something the coachee has said. Often, the response is 'I've never thought of it like that'! It can be surprising to see how some coachees react to their own stories being played back to them. For many, it can seem like it is the first time they have heard an idea – even though the coach is only paraphrasing what the coachee has said. Apparently, there is something quite powerful about having someone else vocalise some of the challenges and situations that are of concern.

In a coaching context, paraphrasing can even use exactly the same words (this is also called 'mirroring'). For our purposes, paraphrasing is therefore the act of capturing something that a coachee says and playing it back to her, in order to elucidate meaning.

Summarising in coaching

At its simplest level, the skill of summarising is about listening attentively to what a coachee says and then playing this back to her succinctly. The key purpose of summarising is to interpret what the coachee has said and present it back to her 'in a nutshell'. As with paraphrasing, summarising can demonstrate that the coach is listening. More importantly, a summary can be used more strategically, to highlight an aspect of what the coachee has said or to reframe the coachee's interpretation of a situation.

Summarising is useful during coaching conversations for the following reasons:

1. It demonstrates that the coach is listening.
2. It allows the coach to check her understanding of what has been said.
3. It can refocus the attention of a conversation.
4. It can be used to reframe the coachee's perception of a situation.

SNAPSHOT   Summarising when coaching

Coachee: 'I'm not as confident at work as I used to be. There's a million reasons for this.'
Coach: 'A million reasons?'
Coachee: 'Well, maybe not a million, but quite a few. Firstly, there are three of us who started here together, in 2002. Both of the others are now in senior manager positions. They've both been promoted twice, and I'm still in the same role. In addition, I've missed some of my performance management targets recently. It may be because of this, or for other reasons, but my line manager has not been very positive about the targets that I do achieve. And even more worryingly, some of my colleagues, who used to do great work, have been made redundant in the last round of cuts. I guess that all of this overshadows the fact that I do work hard and put in the hours. I don't know. It just feels different, and I'm starting to doubt my own abilities.'
Coach: 'Right. So it sounds like you've recently started to question your own abilities because of a number of things that have been happening at work. You're worried that this doubt is starting to overshadow the good work that you are continuing to deliver. Have I understood this correctly?'

Watch Video 5.3 to see summarising in action.

Demonstrating that the coach is listening

A theme of this book is that it is a coach's responsibility to *demonstrate* the necessary skills and 'way of being' when working with a coachee. One way of demonstrating that a coach is listening attentively is to accurately and empathically summarise what the coachee has been saying. A good summary proves beyond doubt that a coach is listening. The fact is, some people are good at *looking* like they are listening. The right noises ('uh huh'), nodding at the right moments, tilting the head sideways – these are useful techniques, but they do not necessarily mean that the coach is genuinely listening.

Checking understanding

An accurate and brief summary of what the coachee has been saying is a good way of minimising the chances of misunderstandings or confusion. This applies to both parties. Sometimes, the coach will not have fully grasped the meaning behind a coachee's explanation. In this situation, a summary is a good way of checking that understanding and can give the coachee an opportunity to clarify what was meant. At other times, a summary can highlight inconsistencies in the coachee's understanding of a situation. In this case, the coachee could reassess her own interpretation of what is happening.

Story from Practice

This example comes from a coaching assignment for a large financial services organisation. The contract was for four coaching sessions of two hours in length. In a pre-coaching meeting with the coachee and his line manager, it became clear that both the coachee and the organisation were hoping that the coaching sessions would lead to a clearer understanding of the coachee's future career plan.

As a result, the first coaching session centred on the coachee's previous career history, his current role and any future plans. As we discussed his current role, he said that it felt like he was on 'train tracks' before we explored how well he felt he was performing within the organisation. Before moving on to explore options, I thought it would be useful to summarise what the coachee had been saying. 'So, you were recruited straight into this organisation from university on a graduate programme about five years ago. You've been performing exceptionally well by your own assessment and that of your line manager and peers. You feel that you're on track with your career, and now you are starting to ask questions about what might come next. Is that a fair summary of where you are?' There was an embarrassed silence before the coachee said kindly that it was 'mostly right'. When he mentioned the train tracks, he did not mean that he was 'on track' in the way that I had understood. What he was trying to convey was the sense that he felt like a train that could only run on tracks. In other words, he felt very restricted, and he wanted coaching so that he could explore whether there might be other directions for him to pursue. Having initially misunderstood the analogy, we were then able to use it correctly, and we talked about the next stations if he were to stay 'on the tracks' and whether there were any junctions that would allow the train to get onto different tracks.

As one of the intentions of summarising is to invite corrections, adaptations or elaborations from the coachee, it is important that a coach's summary is presented in the most tentative way possible. Summaries should not be presented as 'fixed' or certain. For example, 'Right. So that's fairly clear. You only have two options, you've tried one of them already, and you're not prepared to have a go at the other', is less likely to encourage a response than, 'OK. If I've understood correctly, you've identified two options. You've tried one of these, and you're not inclined to try the other. Is that about right?' The tentative nature of the summarising may encourage the coachee to engage with what has been said. Coaches should also think about their style of delivery. Gentle delivery and a tentative tone of voice can enhance the value of summarising.

Refocusing attention

Summaries can be used as a way of managing a conversation and focusing attention on particular aspects of what is being discussed. For example, if a coachee decided to talk about her desire to return to college to study art but spent much of her time talking about how funding for the arts was being cut, summarising might be a helpful way of bringing the conversation back to its original purpose. For example, the coach could say 'OK. So you started by talking about wanting to go back to college to study art. You've also shared your disappointment about funding cuts in this area. Despite this, you seem to be committed to signing up for an art course in September. Have I understood you correctly?'

Reframing

Summaries are helpful when reframing something that a coachee has said for the purposes of highlighting a particular aspect. For example, if a coachee has been talking in general about her career history without recognising the importance of her own successes, the coach could highlight these in the summary: 'So it sounds like you've had a rich career history, including some notable early successes including being elected "young entrepreneur of the year" and then becoming the youngest senior manager within the region.'

In summary

Both paraphrasing and summarising are helpful ways of demonstrating that you are listening to the coachee. They can also be used to check understanding. Summarising is particularly suited to supporting a coachee to refocus attention and reframe her perceptions. Paraphrasing, on the other hand, can helpfully slow down the pace of a coaching session. Many coachees report that they value the 'quality thinking time' that coaching represents. If they feel overwhelmed in the office or pressured by a busy workplace, a coaching conversation which is less harried can create the ideal environment for meaningful reflection.

Often, it is the coach who is carefully summarising and playing back her reflections to the coachee. It may be helpful, on occasion, to pass this task onto the coachee. For example, if the coachee has been talking about a particularly complex topic or a large number of potential opportunities it may be interesting to ask her the following questions: 'Would this be a good point to stop and reflect on what we've covered so far?' or 'Now that we've talked through the current reality, how would you summarise the situation in one or two sentences?'

SNAPSHOT   Some tips when paraphrasing

- To do this well, you must listen attentively to the coachee.
- Select statements or thoughts which seem to have significance to the coachee.
- Do not be afraid of playing back whole phrases or sentences.
- Start with a phrase that makes it obvious what you are going to do: 'Can I just check that back with you?' or 'Is it OK if I just play that back?'
- As far as possible, do not interpret what the coachee has said.

SNAPSHOT   Some tips when summarising

- If you have concerns about your short-term memory, ask permission to take notes during the session.
- Make sure that the summary is a clear, brief version of what the coachee has said.
- Include any unusual words, phrases, similes or metaphors that the coachee has used.
- Include any specific points that the coachee emphasised.
- Sometimes it is helpful to let the coachee know that you will be summarising. For example, 'I think it may be helpful to pause here and summarise what we've talked about so far.'
- Present your summary in a very tentative manner, allowing the coachee every possible opportunity to correct, elaborate or reconsider.
- When corrections are made, do not take this personally. Avoid the temptation to defend your summary.

SNAPSHOT   Useful phrases for summarising and paraphrasing

- 'I wonder if it would be helpful to summarise what you've said...'
- 'What I've understood so far is...'

- 'What I think I've heard you say is…'
- 'Would it be OK to check my understanding of the situation?'
- 'Would I be right in saying that…'
- 'I may be wrong but…'
- 'So it seems that there are a few key issues…'
- 'It would be helpful for me if you could summarise the main points…'

SNAPSHOT   Tentative concluding questions

- 'Did that sound about right?'
- 'Would you say that was a fair summary?'
- 'Have I missed anything?'
- 'Was that an accurate representation of what you said?'

Appropriate interruptions

This is where it can get a bit complicated. Is it ever OK to interrupt your coachee? The answer is 'definitely not' and 'yes, that is part of your role as coach' at the same time! In principle, we must show our coachee respect at all times. This includes not interrupting when she is speaking. This raises a challenge for us as coaches. As we will show later (Chapter 7), the responsibility for managing the coaching *process* rests with the coach. Ensuring that best use is made of the time available is primarily the coach's responsibility. So where does that leave us?

One way to approach this is for coaches to decide beforehand the circumstances in which they might interrupt. I propose below two different types of interruption that are acceptable during coaching conversations.

1. Procedural interruption

The first type relates to interruptions that help to manage the process of the coaching conversation. Timekeeping is the responsibility of the coach and therefore it may at times be necessary to intervene during the conversation to ensure that it comes to an appropriate conclusion. For example, if there are ten minutes remaining in the coaching conversation and the coachee starts to revisit information that was already covered in the early stages, a procedural interruption may be appropriate. All interruptions should begin with an apology and an explanation of why the intervention is being made: 'I'm very sorry to intervene but I have noticed that we have ten minutes remaining for our coaching conversation. Perhaps we can revisit this topic at a future session? For now, I wonder if you would be OK with us focusing on an action plan to implement before the next time we meet?' Other acceptable procedural interruptions can be used to ensure that the coachee is broadly following the agreed coaching process (the GROW coaching process will be discussed in Chapter 7).

2. Emphatic interruption

This phrase refers to the purpose of the interruption (emphasis) rather than the way the coach interrupts. Often, coachees will say something of significance as part of a longer exploration of their current situation or preferred future. There are occasions when the coach may think it helpful to emphasise these points. There will be times when it may be more appropriate to wait until the coachee comes to a natural conclusion. There will also be times when it is helpful to highlight the point straight away. For example, if the coachee has been speaking for a good amount of time and says 'anyway, what I think is not important' and carries on talking, the coach may want to emphasise that assertion in order to explore the origin of that view: 'Sorry to intervene, but I noticed that you said that what you think is not important. I think it may be helpful to explore what made you say that.' Other occasions for emphatic interruptions are when the coachee overlooks or underplays her strengths, talents or resourcefulness. For example, if, as part of a longer explanation about her role in an organisation, a coachee says 'because I led on our successful bid to gain Investors in People recognition, I never had a chance to be involved in...', it may be helpful for the coach to use an emphatic interruption: 'Sorry to intervene at this point, but I'd like to find out a bit more about what you said. What was your involvement with the Investors in People recognition?' This is helpful because it highlights one of the coachee's achievements. Talking about such successes is often motivational and can build energy into a conversation. Videos 5.4 and 5.5 are good examples of how the coach can interrupt emphatically.

Conclusion

In this chapter, we have considered two key skills: paraphrasing and summarising. Both are essential in coaching conversations as they provide a coachee with clear evidence that the coach is listening to her attentively. Paraphrasing is simply repeating back what you have heard, using your own words (or sometimes using the coachee's words). Summarising involves understanding what the coachee has said and playing it back to her in a condensed way. Both are good ways to check our understanding. Coachees should feel comfortable correcting the coach if they think that the paraphrasing or summarising does not accurately capture their meaning. Finally, we briefly considered situations in which it may be acceptable to interrupt the coachee: procedural interruptions when the coach is managing the conversation to get the most benefit from it and emphatic interruptions when it is important to highlight something that the coachee has said straight away. In the next chapter, we will consider another pair of skills: giving and receiving feedback.

6

GIVING AND RECEIVING FEEDBACK

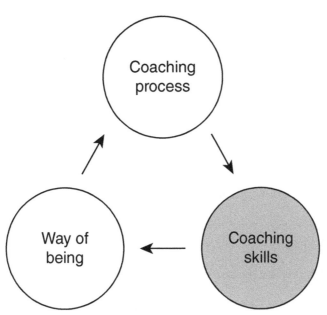

Figure 6.1   The three elements of effective coaching

The final set of skills we shall consider in this book are giving and receiving feedback. To support coachees to achieve more of their potential, coaches must be skilled at giving feedback. To function at their best, coaches need to be able to receive feedback from their coachees.

Giving feedback

Having established that coaching is about learning and development, it follows that a coachee should benefit from timely feedback from her coach. The confidential nature of coaching sessions is ideal for giving honest feedback in a way that a coachee might find acceptable. It may be human nature to become defensive when presented with negative feedback. This is why it is important to build strong, mutually trusting relationships between the coach and coachee. Coaching is often the only safe space for coachees to receive feedback without feeling overly threatened.

What type of feedback can a coach provide?

How much helpful feedback a coach can provide will depend on how well the coach knows the coachee and the level of access to any additional information about her. Even if the coach and the coachee do not know one another at all, the coach can provide feedback about two important factors.

Firstly, it may be helpful to the coachee to know how you experience her as a person. If you, as a coach, experience the coachee in a particular way, it is possible that other people may experience her in similar ways. Secondly, any impressions and thoughts formed through your interactions with the coachee can be a rich source of additional data. While others may experience the coachee in a similar way, they may not be willing or able to share their views.

SNAPSHOT   Feedback to coachees

Based on the coach's experience of meeting the coachee for the first time:

'I found you to be very warm and friendly when we first met. You came downstairs to the reception area to greet me, and made sure that I was offered a cup of coffee before we started.'

Based on coaching conversations:

'When coaching, I've noticed that you are not very expressive. You do not use hand gestures and you did not want to undertake a drawing activity. Even when we were talking about a future aspiration which you said you were excited about, it was not evident through your facial expressions.'

Both pieces of feedback shown above (in the Snapshot box) could be helpful to a coachee. If presented positively within a strong coaching relationship, feedback can raise self-awareness and provide the coachee with valuable information about how others might perceive her. At times, it can be a challenging task to give a coachee accurate feedback. This chapter will provide you with some practical ideas about how to incorporate effective feedback into your coaching practice.

Providing helpful feedback

It may be beneficial at this point to remind ourselves what coaching is all about. The coach's role is to support the coachee to achieve her goals and unlock more of her potential. Often, coachees feel stuck or unable to achieve their goals, but they are not sure what is stopping them. Coaching can be helpful in providing coachees with more information about their strengths and weaknesses as they work towards their goals. One of the responsibilities of the coach is to be honest with the coachee. Morally this is the right thing to do, but it is also a way of building and maintaining a strong relationship with the coachee. Part of this honesty includes providing accurate and timely feedback if this will help the coachee to achieve her goals.

Story from Practice

I was coaching a senior executive who was finding it challenging to manage a change programme within her organisation. It was our first meeting and she declared that her staff were not supportive towards her and were disengaged with the change programme she was leading. This irritated and surprised her. According to the senior executive, she was very accessible and had a clearly stated 'open door policy' which everyone understood. Her goal was to get her team on board in order to make the necessary changes required for the success of the business.

The coachee's perception of how accessible she was differed from my own brief experience of my interactions with her. When attempting to agree the coaching contract, I had been instructed to negotiate diaries with her personal assistant, rather than directly with her. It had proven impossible to have a telephone conversation with the coachee before the meeting despite three separate attempts to coordinate diaries. In the end, I wrote her an introductory email, explaining my coaching style and saying that I was looking forward to meeting. Her response was a short one-line email without any salutation. When I arrived at the coachee's office, I was kept waiting at reception at the front of the building before having to wait again outside her office on the second floor. Although I was there about ten minutes early, her personal assistant informed me that she would be ready to see me at the time of my appointment. It wasn't clear whether the PA had let the coachee know that I had arrived. In other words, my own experience did not confirm the coachee's impression about how accessible she was. In this case, I had some information that could be helpful to the coachee. At this point I asked myself two questions that I always refer to in this situation. The first question is: 'Would this feedback be helpful to the coachee in achieving her goals?' As she was hoping to engage members of her team in a change programme, being easy to contact or speak to would be very important. I concluded that objective feedback from an external coach could be useful additional information for the coachee. The second question is: 'Is this relationship strong enough for me to provide this feedback now?' Having only known the coachee for 30 minutes, I decided that the timing was

(Continued)

(Continued)

not ideal to provide the feedback during that session. However, I made a note about the 'open door policy' and continued to listen to the coachee's description of the current situation. At the end of the first session, the coachee decided that she needed to actively invest in strengthening her relationships with key members of her team.

During the second coaching session, there was an opportunity to share my observations and experiences about coming to see her for the first time. She was surprised to hear of my experiences. Initially, she was slightly defensive, and provided explanations and excuses for her one-line email and the PA's reasons for having kept me waiting. However, she subsequently reflected on this and realised that some of her team members' lack of engagement might be due to difficulties in getting in touch with her.

The story provides an example of a situation in which some data held by the coach might be helpful for the coachee. It also highlights the need for the coach to be courageous about providing this feedback. In the story above, it would have been easier and less risky for the coach to keep his views to himself. Let us consider another case.

Story from Practice

In another coaching assignment, I worked with a number of staff members from a large further education college. Due to the planned retirement of a senior leader at the end of the academic year, the college had asked me to have coaching conversations with some of the potential candidates who might take his place. Interestingly, the senior leader had a designated deputy, but everyone I spoke to seemed to think it unlikely that this person would get the leadership position. 'Nobody takes her seriously', 'There's no way they'd appoint her', 'She's only tolerated because she's been here as long as anyone can remember' were some of the comments mentioned. The way she dressed, her old-fashioned ways (she didn't have a mobile phone), and the way she always talked about how things were better in the past, meant that she wasn't taken seriously by most of the staff. Although I did not have an opportunity to coach this member of staff, I felt that she may have benefitted from some honest feedback. Without this feedback, it would be very difficult for her to achieve her goals or get the respect that she deserved.

What About You?

If you were in the position of this member of staff and you were hoping to get promoted, would you prefer to know what others thought, or would you rather not know?

What do you think prevented staff members from being honest with their colleague?

How can we tell that feedback would be helpful?

There are a number of indications that additional information could be helpful for the coachee:

1. The coachee does not understand why something is happening.
    For example, 'I don't know why I never get selected for interviews for senior leadership positions.' The surprise or lack of understanding suggests that the coachee is missing some information, either about herself or about the situation.
2. The coachee notices that the same situation keeps recurring.
    For example, 'It's the same with every manager I have had. They always take advantage of my good nature.' If a coachee finds herself caught in a cycle or pattern, there is a possibility that she is not aware of her part in the situation.
3. The coachee makes numerous assumptions about what others think.
    For example, 'I think she assumes that I am intimidated because I have only been in the business for less than a year.' Basing actions or responses on untested assumptions is risky.

In each of these cases, it is helpful for the coachee to have more information about what is happening. Often it is simply a case of asking people. For example, a good coaching question to ask a coachee who is uncertain about what others think of her presentations is: 'How can you find out?' Sometimes the coachee will need encouragement to do this. If it is something that she is concerned about, it may well be that she is reluctant to ask because she does not want to hear the answer.

Sources of feedback

While we may agree that feedback is helpful for coachees, we should not assume that the coach is the only person that it can come from. In fact, it is much more likely that the coachee will get her feedback from other sources.

SNAPSHOT   Potential sources of feedback

- Asking colleagues, friends and family
- 360 degree assessment tools
- Psychometric questionnaires
- Performance review meetings
- Being observed
- Video recording

How to collect feedback

Asking colleagues, friends and family

The simplest way of getting feedback is to ask someone for it. Work colleagues can be useful sources of information. For example, if a manager feels that team meetings are not valued by members of her team, it makes sense to ask them directly. Some will prefer to go to people they trust or have an existing relationship with. Others will be comfortable to talk to anyone. Often, coachees will resist this approach, saying that they think that they will not get truthful feedback. Firstly, this is an assumption. Secondly, some feedback which may be dubious is better than no feedback at all.

360 degree assessment tool

A more robust and generally accepted way of collecting work-related data is the 360 degree assessment tool. These are usually externally-administered questionnaires which are completed by a number of staff in an organisation. A questionnaire is sent to the person concerned as well as her line manager, peers and direct reports. Recipients are asked questions about the person's competencies and behaviours. The assessment tool generates a report that collates all the responses, providing some quantitative data and some qualitative data. The 360 degree assessment tool can be helpful because it provides an external view of the person based on multiple responses. From a coaching perspective, the report provides a very good starting point for discussion. Differences between the coachee's self-assessment and the responses of others would be an area of particular interest.

Psychometric questionnaires

Coachees can be asked to complete psychometric questionnaires. Many are now available online and can measure a whole range of attributes, skills and strengths. In all self-report questionnaires, the feedback is based on the information provided by the coachee. The reports produced by psychometric questionnaires also provide a starting point for coaching discussions. Again, any results that are surprising to the coachee may be a focus for further exploration.

Performance review meetings

The notes of performance review meetings between the coachee and her line manager can contain useful feedback. Coachees can take advantage of performance review meetings to solicit clear and explicit feedback.

Being observed

Some executive coaches offer to observe their coachees in the workplace. This can create a link between the coaching room and the place of work. However, even with the attendance of a coach, the feedback is still being generated by someone else and it is not as powerful as allowing the coachee to see herself in her professional role.

Video recording

Video recording oneself is also a very powerful way of getting feedback. As there is no interpretation at all, it is difficult for a coachee to reject the feedback that she is seeing with her own eyes. Very often, we do not know what it looks like when we do what we do. When using video with coachees, it is recommended that they are given time to watch the clip for themselves first. This gives them a chance to get used to seeing themselves on a screen so that they will be able to focus on the changes they want to make when they meet with a coach.

It's not what you say, it's how you say it

In coaching, it is always more important to consider how to convey feedback than the content of the feedback itself. The feedback should never be diluted. Coaches should instead concentrate on two factors: the strength of the coaching relationship and the clarity of the information provided. If the relationship is strong enough, it can be argued that the coachee can accept any feedback, however challenging it may be. For this reason, a coach should assess the quality and strength of the coaching relationship before sharing negative feedback with the coachee. Fearing the response of others, people sometimes water down the feedback that is provided. This is ultimately counterproductive as the feedback will start to lack clarity.

SNAPSHOT   Watered down feedback that starts to lack clarity

Feedback received following a presentation: 'I'm not sure how to put it. Your presentation was interesting, and some people seemed to get something practical out of it. Maybe it wasn't to everyone's taste. But overall, I think it did the job.'

In the example above, hesitation about 'how to put it' and the use of the ambiguous word 'interesting' can lead to uncertainty about the real message. By suggesting that 'some people'

(Continued)

(Continued)

seemed to get something out of it, there is an implied suggestion that others did not. The same applies to the comment that it 'wasn't to everyone's taste'. The term 'maybe' throws the whole sentence into question. Finally, the attempt to end on a positive note ('overall, I think it did the job') further clouds the meaning and intention of the feedback. Not only is the feedback confusing, it provides very little practical information about what changes could be made.

The same effect occurs when negative feedback is couched between patronising positive comments.

SNAPSHOT   Sugarcoating negative feedback

'Firstly, I want to say that I like the way you never give up with things. This presentation did not go well. It missed the point and you did not talk about what people were expecting to hear. But, on a positive front, your presentation looked very pretty.'

The recipient of the 'feedback sandwich' is left unsure whether she has received positive or negative feedback. The real problem is that people often make up something positive to say just to counterbalance the negative feedback. Instead of creating a balanced feel, the positive feedback can come across as insincere. Most of us like positive feedback, and we deserve to get this without it having to act as a counterbalance to negative feedback.

When providing feedback in coaching sessions it is important to remember that the feedback should be objective and specific. The coachee needs to understand what information is being provided and it must not be the personal perception of the coach. Rather, it should be verifiable facts presented in an objective way. The coachee should derive her own conclusions from the feedback provided.

SNAPSHOT   Clear and specific feedback

Coach: 'Would you like some honest feedback about the presentation?'
Coachee: 'Yes, please.'
Coach: 'Great. I want to provide you with my observations about the presentation so that we can work on ways of improving your practice.'
Coachee: 'Yes, that's OK. Hit me with it!'
Coach: 'Firstly, your presentation topic did not match what was advertised in the promotional material. Secondly, while two or three people near the front of the

room asked questions and took notes, most of the other delegates seemed less engaged, not looking at the handouts and not sharing their thoughts. Finally, I noticed that five or six of the delegates left before you had finished. What is your interpretation of what happened?'

It is important, as a coach, to get agreement from the coachee before providing negative feedback. Once the feedback has been provided, it is appropriate to ask the coachee to respond. A critical factor for both parties (coach and coachee) is that the intention of the feedback is clear. As coaching is an intervention which supports coachees to achieve their goals, this should be implied already. However, there is no harm in reiterating the positive intention of delivering negative feedback before doing so.

When to provide feedback

As we showed in one of the 'stories from practice' above, the timing of providing feedback is critical to its success. There are times in a relationship when it is not helpful to provide clear feedback. Simply put, as human beings there are times when we are less open to feedback. For example, just after someone has completed a presentation may not be the best time to provide the speaker with negative feedback. The same person might be much more receptive to feedback later in the day. In a coaching context, the timing is linked to the strength of the relationship. Negative feedback is best provided after a good relationship has been established.

Ratio of interaction

Positive feedback is also very important in coaching conversations. Coaches are strengths-finders, and therefore should be listening for strengths, achievements and positive attributes. It is helpful for a person's self-esteem and morale if a coach reflects these back during a coaching session. Often, coachees can be quite modest about their achievements, and at other times may not realise that they have achieved something out of the ordinary. As long as this is done in an honest and genuine way, a coach's feedback about what is positive can make a difference to her coachee.

Research undertaken by Frederickson and Losada (2005) suggests that human beings are more likely to flourish if they experience a ratio of three positive emotions to one negative emotion. Therefore, it is important that we, as coaches, provide a similar ratio of positive to negative (or constructive) feedback to our coachees. In fact, Losada and Heaphy (2004) undertook research with management teams in organisations and discovered that feedback was most effective at a ratio of three instances of positive feedback to one instance of negative feedback. This positive effect applied to the 3:1 ratio and above, but tailed off when the ratio exceeded 11:1.

This provides coaches with a useful insight. We should balance our feedback to our coachees, favouring positive and encouraging comments and observations. I call this a 'bias towards the positive'. However, to ensure that our feedback is most effective, it is important to remember that some negative or constructive feedback is also desirable.

See how coaches can identify positives and feed these back to their coachees by watching Videos 6.2 and 6.3.

What About You?

How do you respond to feedback? What would be your response to continuous, positive feedback (with no negative or constructive feedback at all)?

Demonstrating openness to feedback

Receiving feedback is an important part of a coach's development. It is also a prime opportunity for the coach to demonstrate openness to feedback. Following each session, it is recommended that the coach seek feedback from the coachee (see Videos 6.4 and 6.5). This provides the coach with an opportunity to evaluate her practice and it models a positive approach to feedback. It is normal for the coach to feel defensive if she receives negative feedback. However, in this case, the coachee's perceptions of what happened are very important to the coach. If the coach receives negative feedback, she should refrain from providing excuses. Instead, she should listen carefully to what is being said and take the information away to reflect on it, perhaps during a supervisory conversation.

Learning from feedback

A significant part of human learning comes from feedback. Some would go as far as to suggest that we are unable to learn without it. As a coach, it is important to demonstrate this. When receiving feedback it is important to be calm and look interested and responsive. Rather than justifying or defending certain behaviours, a coach should use her listening skills to hear what is being said. It is almost a certainty that if a coach responds badly to feedback from a coachee, that person is very unlikely to provide any further feedback in future.

This is not to say that all feedback provided by anyone should automatically be accepted as correct. Initially, however, it is important that people are as open as possible to all sources of information that may help them to achieve more than they are currently achieving. Once the information has been heard, it is possible to reflect on it and consider an appropriate response. There are essentially only two simple responses as shown in Table 6.1.

Table 6.1   Ways in which we can respond to feedback

I accept that this feedback is accurate	
a Accurate and straightforward	'I can start to make changes'
b Accurate but difficult	'I know I need to make changes but it's painful'
c Accurate but unsure how to proceed	'I agree with the feedback but I do not know what to do'
I do not accept that this feedback is accurate	
a Inaccurate and straightforward	'I can reject the feedback because it is inaccurate'
b Inaccurate and misleading	'The person giving me the feedback has an ulterior motive, so the feedback can be rejected'
c Inaccurate but complicated	'The feedback may be wrong but it highlights other issues such as the relationship between myself and the person providing the feedback, so it cannot be rejected completely'

This means that feedback needs to be first listened to and then considered as objectively as possible. After consideration, a decision can be taken. It is perfectly acceptable to listen carefully to feedback, consider its validity and then reject it outright as long as there are good reasons to do so.

Taking it personally

Many people withhold feedback out of a fear that others will take it personally. I believe that this is inevitable, especially if the feedback relates to something related to a person's sense of self. For example, if a teacher receives negative feedback about what she does, it is not reasonable to expect her *not* to take it personally. Evidently, a teacher's sense of self will be closely entwined with how well she does her job. This applies to well-intentioned feedback as well as malicious feedback. As coaches, we must accept that an initial, defensive reaction to feedback is normal. The coaching session can provide a safe space for a coachee to take in the feedback without feeling self-conscious, or under threat. This makes a coaching session one of the best contexts for delivering helpful feedback.

What About You?

How good are you at accepting feedback? Do you know what others think of your ability in your various roles? Why not ask for feedback?

Having considered the skills of coaching, we will now turn our attention to a coaching process.

PART THREE
COACHING PROCESS

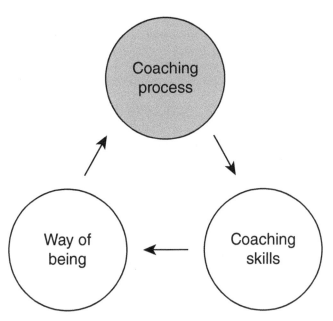

Figure 7.1 The three elements of effective coaching

Having surveyed some of the key coaching skills, let us turn our attention to the coaching process. In 1992, Sir John Whitmore popularised a coaching process which was to transform the profession and become one of the best-known coaching models. Simple, but not simplistic, the GROW model will be presented in this book as a framework for your coaching practice. It is important, at this stage, to emphasise that the GROW model is *one* coaching process out of many that are now available for coaches.

GROW is an acronym of the four words representing the different stages of the process: Goal, Reality, Options and Will (Whitmore, 1992). The strength of the model is that the GROW process increases the likelihood of a conversation which leads to change. It was originally devised as a behavioural coaching model. This means that the process was created to support conversations about behavioural change – helping coachees to *do* something differently. However, the GROW model lends itself to cognitive behavioural approaches as well. In other words, it can be used to help people to change their cognitions as well as their behaviour – helping people to *think* and *act* differently. The cognitive behavioural aspect of coaching will be discussed in the next chapter (Chapter 8). The GROW model has been heavily imitated with many authors proposing alternative sets of letters and finding new words to describe each of the stages. In one way, these can be considered endorsements of the original GROW process.

While you have the choice to select a preferred coaching model, or even create your own, there are two key points that should be addressed before we proceed.

1. A coaching conversation *must* follow a process.
2. The purpose of coaching is to support goal-setting and attainment.

Over decades of research, writers and academics in the fields of counselling and coaching have invested significant effort in trying to prove that a particular intervention or approach is more effective than another. This has not yet been proven, so we can tentatively work on the assumption that there is no one coaching process that is the 'right' one. However, it has been shown that a coach's (or counsellor's) belief in her chosen process has a significant impact on the perceived success of coaching partnerships (de Haan, 2008b).

At heart, coaching is an interaction that supports people to achieve goals. In a sense, the desire to achieve something, overcome a barrier, or fulfil an ambition is what brings people to coaching. One of the leading figures in the field of coaching psychology, Dr Anthony M. Grant, is clear and emphatic: 'all coaching conversations are either explicitly or implicitly goal-focused' (2012: 149).

If you remember, it was suggested in the introduction that novice coaches should address three elements of coaching as part of their learning journeys. The first element is the set of skills needed. We've already discussed the skills of listening, asking questions, paraphrasing, summarising, giving feedback and receiving feedback. In this section, we will be considering the second necessary element: the coaching process.

Most coaching conversations last between 30 minutes and 2 hours. If you use the GROW process, there are certain stages that should be followed. Each of these is listed below, with questions which capture the general focus of each stage:

Goal: What would you like to achieve?
Reality (current reality): What is the current situation (in relation to what you have identified as a goal)?
Options (generating options): What options can you think of (that will help you to move closer to your goal)?
Will (way forward): What will you do as a result of the coaching session?

SNAPHOT   GROW model

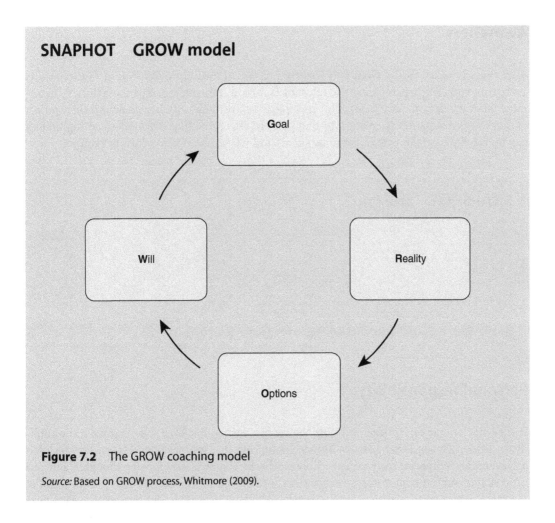

Figure 7.2   The GROW coaching model

Source: Based on GROW process, Whitmore (2009).

According to Whitmore (2009), coaching has two main intentions: to raise awareness and develop a sense of personal responsibility. He proposes that coaching should raise the *coachee's* awareness about her situation and should instil a sense of personal responsibility. In other words, a coachee should be supported to view her situation differently so that she realises that she is able to move towards her goals.

SNAPSHOT   The two intentions of every coaching session

- Raising the awareness of the coachee
- Encouraging the coachee to take personal responsibility

Awareness

Awareness is raised in the **Goal** and **Reality** phases. According to Whitmore, 'awareness' is 'gathering and clearly perceiving the relevant facts and information, and the ability to determine what is relevant' (2009: 34). The coachee is asked to identify her goal, and then reflect on her current situation in relation to that goal. In effect, the first two stages can highlight a gap between where she would like to be (goal) and where she is now (current reality).

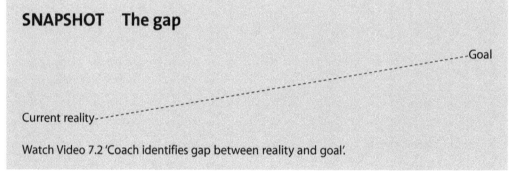

SNAPSHOT   The gap

Goal

Current reality

7.2

Watch Video 7.2 'Coach identifies gap between reality and goal'.

Personal responsibility

In the latter two stages, **Options** and **Will**, the coachee is encouraged to take personal responsibility for working towards her goals. Whitmore points out that responsibility is necessary for high achievement: 'When we truly accept, choose, or take responsibility for our thoughts and our actions, our commitment to them rises and so does our performance' (2009: 37). This is one of the reasons that it is important for the *coachee* to identify possible options before selecting a specific and explicit way forward. The coachee should also commit to a self-selected action as a result of the coaching session.

Coach and coachee responsibilities

Coaching is a shared enterprise between coach and coachee, and each has responsibilities within the conversation. The coachee should be entirely responsible for the 'content' of the coaching conversation. This means that she should select the topic for the conversation, identify her own goals and the timeframes in which she would like to achieve these. In the meantime, the coach is responsible for managing the 'process' of the coaching conversation (in this case, the GROW process). The coach must manage the time allocated for the conversation, help the coachee to stay focused on her goal and take an interest in progress. In this way, it is clear that both parties have different roles during coaching. Let us consider the GROW model now, as an overall process, looking briefly at each stage (watch Video 7.3).

Stages of the GROW process

Goal

The first stage facilitates the selection and discussion of the coachee's goals. We are interested in finding out what the coachee seeks to achieve through coaching. What has motivated the coachee to seek coaching, and what does she want as an outcome?

Reality

The second stage provides the coachee with an opportunity to explain the current situation. At the same time, this offers the coach a way of building rapport and demonstrating empathy. The relationship between the 'current reality' and the agreed goals can be explored in this phase.

Options

This stage moves the process from a focus on 'raising awareness' to a conversation which encourages the coachee to take 'personal responsibility'. The main outcome of this stage is a self-identified way forward selected out of a range of options.

Will

The final stage, crucial for the success of a coaching conversation, requires the coachee to commit to a next step. Coach and coachee work together to identify what the coachee will *do* as a result of the conversation.

Let us now consider the process in more detail.

Goal stage

Grant has provided us with interesting, evidence-based theories of goal-setting and attainment. As coaching is a goal-centred intervention, this work is directly relevant. According to Grant, it is important to set **short-term** (proximal) and **long-term** (distal) goals to aid long-term performance (2012). Locke and Latham found that goals that are **stretching** *and* **achievable** can lead to high performance (2002). If a goal is too easy, it is no longer motivating. So that people can tell when they have achieved their goals, it is helpful if those goals are measurable (**outcome** goals) (Locke, 1996). Finally, and perhaps most significantly for coaches, it has been suggested that goals should be **self-selected.** Deci and Ryan have shown that people are more committed to goals which they have chosen to pursue (rather than goals which are imposed by others) (2002). It is the coach's role to manage the **Goal** phase so that the coachee can select relevant and meaningful goals (watch Video 7.4).

It is crucial to recognise that different types of goals should be discussed and agreed during this phase. The first is the 'overall goal' or aspiration that has brought the coachee to the conversation. In other words, what does the coachee hope to achieve by being coached? Whitmore calls this an 'end goal', describing it as the 'final objective' (2009: 59). Usually, it is this goal that provides the motivation. The second goal, which is the topic of the coaching conversation, should focus on what the coachee would like to do to move closer to the 'end goal'. Whitmore terms this a 'performance goal' (2009: 59). This should be perceived to be something that the coachee is able to achieve (or is at least within her control). Finally, it is important for coaches to clarify what the coachee would like to achieve during the coaching conversation. This should be very specific.

The coach has an interest in ensuring that this goal is achievable within the given time constraints. Take a moment to watch Videos 7.5, 7.6, 7.7 and 7.8.

SNAPSHOT   Sample questions (Goal)

What are you building towards?
What would be the best use of our time together?
What is it you would like to achieve?
What is your desired outcome?
What would you like to achieve during this coaching conversation?
What are your aspirations?

Reality phase

The **Reality** phase allows the coachee to clarify the current situation and creates an opportunity for the coach to strengthen her relationship with the coachee by demonstrating active listening and empathy. As a novice coach, it may be helpful to focus your attention on *listening* to the coachee rather than trying to understand the situation in order to offer a solution. This is a common trap as many of us are trained to listen for 'problems' in order to try to identify 'solutions'. In fact, many novice coaches report that 'having the answer' can get in the way of genuine listening.

See how the coach encourages the coachee to explore her current reality in Video 7.9.

To keep your mind busy during this phase, it may be helpful to focus on your practice as a coach. Effective and experienced coaches may seem to be 'just listening' during the **Reality** phase, but they are actually doing much more in the background:

Demonstrating active listening

The skill of listening has been covered in Chapter 3. It is in the **Reality** phase that it can make the most significant difference. Instead of listening to 'come up with an answer', the experienced coach will listen to create a 'thoughtful' space for the coachee. Even more important than listening in this way is to **demonstrate** that you are listening actively through your attitude and behaviours. A good question to ask yourself when reflecting on your practice is not 'how well did I listen?' but 'what evidence did I provide to the coachee that I was listening?'

Asking open questions

The **Reality** phase is primarily an opportunity for the coachee to share her experiences. This is the phase where the coach should do the least talking. Having said that, an experienced coach will ensure that most interventions are presented as open questions, as these encourage further reflection and exploration. A good question to ask yourself when reflecting on your practice is 'how did my questions help the coachee to do her best thinking?'

Avoiding leading questions

Leading questions have no place in effective coaching conversations. In many ways, these questions are manipulative, insinuating how the coach believes the coachee should behave. A good coach will first notice that she is asking leading questions, then stop herself from asking such questions. With time and with the appropriate 'way of being' (which will be discussed in Chapters 14 and 15), the desire to suggest ways forward through the use of leading questions will diminish. Two good questions to ask yourself when reflecting on your practice are 'Did I ask any leading questions?' and 'What do I have to change so that I am not seeking to find solutions for the coachee?'

Being aware of the process

As explained earlier, the GROW model is one process of many. However, a coach should keep the process in mind while coaching. While it is presented in a linear fashion, the GROW model is cyclical and flexible. Often, a coachee may want to return to the **Goal** stage to refine her goal. At other times, the coach may need to return to the **Goal** stage to renegotiate the focus of the conversation with the coachee. At all times, the experienced coach will be aware of where the conversation is in relation to the GROW process. As stated earlier, as a coach, the process is your responsibility. So depending on the length of the session, the coach should be thinking about how much time should be spent on each stage, including the **Reality** phase. A good question to ask yourself when reflecting on your practice is 'What interventions did I make to ensure that our conversation followed a recognised process?'

Ensuring an appropriate focus on the goal

The **Reality** stage is the coachee's opportunity to 'offload' or 'paint a picture' of what things are like for her. The coach's role is to listen attentively, and also to ensure that there is a link between the context that is described and the goal that has been selected. A good way of doing this is to ask the coachee about the relevance of what she has been talking about. For example, 'How does this relate to your goal of achieving a better work-life balance?' Often, there is a relationship, and it is helpful for the coachee to express this link. At other times, the coachee may realise that she has pursued another avenue of thinking that does not relate directly to the selected goal. At this point, it is helpful for the coach to reflect back to the coachee that there is a 'disconnect' between what is being discussed and her stated goal. The coachee can either refocus on the original goal or else select a different goal as the topic for the coaching conversation. In these situations, it is important to explicitly renegotiate this with the coachee. For example, 'It sounds like you have identified another goal. Shall we set the original goal to one side and spend our time talking about this goal instead?' A good question to ask yourself when reflecting on your practice is, 'What interventions did I make to ensure that the conversation focused on the coachee's stated goal?'

Listening for 'facts'

During the **Reality** phase, a coach should remain alert for statements that are presented as 'facts'. For our purposes, we will define a fact 'as a statement or observation that is verifiable'. For example, these could be facts: 'I was born in 1982'; 'My company employs 240 people'; 'There are only three other people involved in the applications process.' This type of information can (theoretically) be verified by checking with other sources of data. However, other statements may be presented as facts when they are not: 'No one in my team will ever support that initiative'; 'In my organisation, you will not get promoted unless you are one of the boss's favourites'; 'People are motivated by self-interest.' Each of these can be presented as 'facts' when they are actually beliefs or assumptions. This becomes a problem when the so-called 'fact' limits the coachee or gets in the way of what she wants to achieve.

Noticing emotions

During the coaching conversation, the coach has an opportunity to listen carefully in order to gather information about emotions that the coachee may be experiencing. This can be done by making a mental note of any mentions of emotions during the conversation – but also by noticing the coachee's posture, body language and mood. The **Reality** stage is an ideal setting for the coachee to reflect on the situation that she is in – and often a chance to talk about how she is feeling about this. If the coachee does not mention emotions at all, the coach could ask 'How do you feel about this situation?' (watch Video 7.10). Helping the coachee to identify the relationship between her goal and the current reality in relation to that goal *and* how she feels about the gap between the two can be the core of the conversation during the **Reality** stage.

Observing body language

Noticing the coachee's body language is another way of keeping our minds busy. Much has been written about body language (this will be discussed in more detail in Chapter 10). In coaching, we can use our knowledge of body language as one source of information to supplement what we know about the coachee. Of course, it is necessary to be very tentative about any information derived in this way. If a coachee crosses her arms, it may be that she is feeling defensive. But it could also suggest that it is cold where you are meeting, that the coachee is angry about an earlier conversation or that she feels comfortable with her arms folded in that way. Often, the most helpful way to use observations about body language is to share them with the coachee: 'I noticed that you were very animated when you talked about the possibility of leading the finance team. You were sitting up straight and using your hands when describing your ideas' (see Video 7.11). This is one way of demonstrating that you are listening that can support the coachee to raise her levels of self-awareness. At the same time, the coachee can correct any misinterpretations of body language.

While it is good practice to notice the body language of a coachee, the coach may also benefit from being mindful about her own non-verbal communications. Nodding is helpful, but overdoing it can have a negative effect. Excessive nodding can make the coachee feel rushed – or even as if she is talking to someone who is trying to 'sell' her something. Leaning backwards in a chair may help the coach's posture but may imply a lack of interest in what the coachee is saying.

SNAPSHOT   Sample questions (Reality)

What is happening at the moment?
How do others perceive this situation?
What are the benefits of this situation?
What is getting in the way of resolving this situation?
How similar is this to situations you have faced before?
What feedback have you had about the current situation?
What do you really do well?
What have you achieved already?

Options stage

The **Options** stage is the one which should be led mostly by the coachee. Paradoxically, it is also the time when most coaches will have to work hardest. By now, the coachee's goals should be clear and the current reality will have been discussed. There is likely to be a gap between what the coachee hopes to achieve and where she perceives herself to be at present.

Watch how the coach carefully moves the conversation from the Reality to the Options stage and how they explain the Options stage in Videos 7.12 and 7.13.

Generating options

At this point, the coachee should be encouraged to think about ways of moving closer to her goal by generating as many options as possible. Tools and techniques for helping to generate creative ideas are discussed in Chapters 11–13. It is important for the coach to push the coachee to identify as many options as possible. It has been suggested that the 'quantity of options is more important at this stage than the quality and feasibility of each one' (Whitmore, 2009: 79). In some cases, a coachee can change her self-perception from victim ('I have no control') to actor ('I can choose my own destiny') simply by realising that she has many options.

Evaluating options

Once many options have been identified, the coach should work with the coachee to evaluate these options. While having a number of choices can be empowering, too many choices can be counter-productive (Iyengar, 2011; Schwartz, 2004). The evaluation criteria should be selected by the coachee. In other words, the coachee should decide how she will choose the best option to pursue. Sometimes this can be done by asking the coachee which option is the simplest to implement, the most likely to result in a positive outcome or the most desirable. At other times, it may be more helpful to go down the list of options, assessing the pros and cons of each. There will also be occasions when a more structured process feels appropriate. In this case, the coachee can create a grid identifying some criteria to apply to each option. For example, a coachee might want to think about her future career options with reference to 'job security', 'work–life balance', 'how fun the job is', 'the pay' and 'status'. In this case, the career options could be entered along the first column, and the criteria across the top of the grid. The coachee could then rate (on a scale of 1–10), each criterion. This would allow for a 'mathematical' calculation of the desirability of each option.

See Video 7.14 and the example of a coachee-initiated evaluation form on the Companion Website (**www.sagepub.co.uk/vannieuwerburgh**).

SNAPSHOT   Sample questions (Options)

What are your options?
What could you do?
What else could you do?
If you could do anything, what would you do?
If you were to advise a friend who faced the same situation, what would you suggest?
What could really unlock this situation for you?
How would someone you really admire deal with this situation?
What is your heart telling you?
What is your head telling you?

Will stage

This is the last phase of the GROW process. Now that the coachee has selected the options she wishes to pursue, it is simply a case of checking for levels of commitment and agreeing to an action plan. At this stage, the coachee should be encouraged to commit to her next steps, using SMART objectives. The SMART acronym (Specific, Measurable, Attainable, Realistic and Timebound) is said to have originated from different authors but attributed to Raia (1965) by Grant (2012). Using this acronym will help the coachee to set realistic, easily measurable tasks before the next coaching session. The coach's role is to seek precision in this stage: Exactly what will the coachee do? When will she do this by? How will she know she has accomplished it? How likely is she to achieve this?

Assessing intention to act

If we accept that behavioural coaching is all about supporting a person to change how she acts in order to help her to achieve her goals, then being able to assess her 'intention to act' is a necessary skill for coaches. Through a combination of what a coachee says, the emotions she expresses and information gathered from her body language, the experienced coach is able to make informed judgements about how likely she is to proceed with an action that she has identified. For example, if a coachee is engaged throughout a session, sits forwards when deciding what needs to happen and is avidly writing down notes about her next steps, her 'intention to act' may be perceived as high. On the other hand, if the coachee looks despondent throughout, has her arms crossed, refuses to write anything down and spends most of her time looking down at her feet, it is not likely that she will proceed with any action that is agreed. Ultimately, it is impossible to know whether a coachee will undertake the actions that she has identified but a subjective assessment of 'intention to act' can sometimes encourage the coach to check a coachee's level of commitment. If there is a discrepancy between the level of commitment and the proposed task, the coach can either work with the coachee to raise the level of commitment or select a less challenging task. It is important that the coachee leaves the coaching conversation motivated and hopeful that she will be able to achieve the task that she has set herself.

Assessing readiness

Throughout the conversation, and especially during the **Will** stage, coaches should be considering the 'readiness' of their coachees. In other words, using all of the information available (body language, mood, what is said, punctuality) the coach should consider how open the coachee is to addressing the topic or issue that is under discussion. For example, if a coachee has been directed to receive coaching, there is a good chance that she may not be 'ready' to be coached. Equally, if a coachee has a headache or is otherwise unwell, she is less likely to benefit from the discussion. Of course, it may be helpful for the coach to check her own level of 'readiness' prior to the start of coaching sessions.

SNAPSHOT   Sample questions (Will)

What will you do?
What is the first step that should be taken?
How will you know that you have succeeded?
What will happen if you achieve your goal?
What will not happen if you achieve your goal?
How committed are you to the actions that you have identified on a scale of 1–10?

Activity   Coaching practice

There is only one way of becoming a coach. That is by coaching. To use the analogy of learning to drive, the only way to pass your test is to practise! And, just like learning how to drive, the GROW process may seem a bit clunky at first. However, we have all been through the initial stages of learning the coaching skills and process. So put on your 'L' plates, and start coaching others. When you are learning:

- stick to the GROW process, ensuring that you are able to manage a conversation from start to finish;
- avoid the temptation to give advice or propose solutions;
- be clear with your coachee that you are still learning how to coach;
- if you have the good fortune to be learning coaching with someone else, coach each other;
- if you are courageous enough, film yourself coaching so that you can reflect on your practice.

Just like driving, once you have mastered the basics, the process will feel smoother. You will then be in a position to adapt the process, add your own techniques and make decisions about when and how to share your own experiences. Until then, please follow the process as closely as possible!

See how the coach explains the GROW process to the coachee in Video 7.15.

Additions to the GROW process

The GROW process is one of the best-known models in the field. As a result, a few adaptations have been suggested, and are noted briefly here.

(T)GROW

Proposed by Miles Downey (2003), the letter 'T' is added to the process. This encourages coaches and coachees to start by discussing the overal 'topic' for coaching. By discussing the topic first, there is less pressure to dive straight into talking about the goal. It can be particularly helpful when the additional stage allows the coachee to talk about her values and aspirations. This would support the coachee to identify goals that are congruent. Such self-concordant goals which are 'in alignment with the coachee's core personal values or developing interests are more likely to be engaging and elicit greater effort' (Grant, 2012: 152).

GROW(TH)

An educational coaching training provider, Growth Coaching International, has adopted the 'GROWTH' model. Building on the effectiveness of the GROW model, the 'T' and the 'H' are added to ensure that new practices are embedded. The 'T' is for tactics. In this phase, the coachee is asked to consider how and when she will undertake the tasks that she has identified. The 'H' phase (habits) is designed to help the coachee consider how she will maintain the new behaviour and turn it into a habit. The GROWTH model is preceded by a phase of building a trusting relationship and concludes with a phase called 'celebrating the results'.

(RE)GROW

In order to emphasise the iterative process required for successful coaching, some practitioners add Review ('R') and Evaluation ('E') to the beginning of the process. This allows for the modification of goals during a series of coaching sessions. The process of reviewing, evaluating and modifying goals can lead to a cycle of self-regulation that can enhance the chances of successful behaviour change (Grant, 2003).

The flexibility of the GROW process

As we can see from a quick survey of adaptations, the GROW process can be redesigned to suit different circumstances. It is a well-known and robust model that has stood the test of time and can be a helpful framework for your coaching practice. As you get familiar with the skills, process and 'way of being' of coaching, you may want to make your own alterations.

Coaching contract

Before embarking on any coaching, it is important for you, as a coach, to establish a coaching contract. The coaching contract should set out how the coach and the coachee will work together. This should be undertaken before starting on the GROW process. Remember, even if the topic is of a personal nature, coaching is a professional conversation. The coaching contract is a great way of establishing the professional parameters of the conversation.

Some coaches have written contracts that they ask their coachees to sign (see the sample on the Companion Website (**www.sagepub.co.uk/vannieuwerburgh**)). Others simply discuss the contract verbally with the coachee at the beginning of the coaching relationship (see Videos 7.16 and 7.17). Good practice is to refer to the coaching contract at every session.

SNAPSHOT   What can be included in a coaching contract

Table 7.1   What to include in a coaching contract

Topic	Specific examples	Importance
Operational issues	• Number of coaching sessions • Length of time per session • Location of meetings • Date of meetings	Recommended
Shared understanding of 'coaching'	• Check that you and the coachee are expecting the same kind of interaction • Clarify the difference between coaching and mentoring • Clarify the difference between coaching and counselling	Recommended
Financial arrangements	• Agree fees for coaching (per session or for the entire contract) • Explain when payment is due • Explain how payments will be made	Essential (if charging for coaching)
Agreement about withdrawal	• Agree how each party might be able to pull out of the coaching arrangement • Agree whether reasons should be given	Recommended
Ethical conduct	• Explain what code of conduct will apply • Declare which professional association the coach is a member of	Essential
Confidentiality	• Be specific about the rules of confidentiality • Explain when confidentiality may be broken (usually, this includes situations when the coach believes that the coachee or others are at risk of harm or when the coachee divulges an illegal activity)	Essential

Topic	Specific examples	Importance
Competence	• Be explicit about your level of experience • Be clear about your boundaries (in relation to counselling)	Recommended
Permissions	• Seek permission for taking notes (and explain what they are for) • Seek permission to interrupt (if you will be doing so) • Seek permission to challenge (if you will be doing so)	Personal preference
Personal style	• Share with the coachee how you work as a coach (e.g. 'non-directive', 'challenging')	Personal preference

Drafting your own coaching contract   Activity

At this stage it is sufficient to draft your coaching contract. What would you like to agree on before starting the coaching? What is it important for the coachee to know? Make some notes in your learning journal.

Conclusion

In this chapter we have considered the GROW coaching process. Each step has been discussed and sample questions have been provided. While you have a choice of coaching models, it is essential to utilise a process when coaching. We have also highlighted the importance of agreeing a contract before any coaching conversation. The necessity of a coaching contract will be revisited in Chapter 16.

8
BEYOND BEHAVIOUR: EXPLORING OUR THINKING

There are times when it may be necessary to move beyond talking simply about behaviours during coaching conversations. The GROW process discussed in the previous chapter was first popularised by Whitmore in *Coaching for Performance* (1992). Whitmore brought welcome attention to the relationship between coaching and performance in a way that made coaching very appealing to the world of business. Based on Whitmore's book, it seemed that coaching held the promise of improved performance of employees, which would, in turn, lead to greater profitability.

Initially, there was an understandable assumption in organisations that staff performance would be enhanced by focusing on behavioural change. Much of the support and evidence for this view derived from the work of behavioural psychologists (see Snapshot) and this approach has been dubbed 'behavioural coaching'. Some would argue that the GROW model is best suited for behavioural coaching (e.g. Passmore, 2007; Alexander, 2010). It is true that the final stage of the GROW process ('What will you **do** differently?') seems to focus on a behavioural outcome.

SNAPSHOT   Behavioural psychology

Behavioural psychology is a branch of psychology that focused on studying observable human behaviours. Behaviourists such as John Watson, Ivan Pavlov, and B.F. Skinner believed in a scientific approach to studying psychology. They argued that the scientific study of 'consciousness' was impossible, advocating instead that psychologists should study behavioural adaptation and the relationship between stimuli and responses (Banyard, Davies, Norman and Winder, 2010).

In Chapter 1, we discussed definitions. The intention of coaching is to lead to a change in behaviour, *or a way of thinking*. The reason I have added 'or a way of thinking' is because sometimes people have to change the way they think before they can alter what they do, especially if they are trying to make long-lasting changes. There has been a long-running, interesting and still unresolved debate about the best way of bringing about sustainable change in human behaviour. The view that both behaviour *and* thinking should be addressed is called the cognitive-behavioural approach.

The question is: 'Should coachees change their behaviours *first*, which would bring about a change in the way they think, or does it work better if coachees start by changing the way they think, which will then lead to changes in how they behave?' There is no need to resolve this question here. In my own experience as a coach, I have seen beneficial and sustainable change being embraced by coachees using both approaches.

In my view, an understanding of psychological theories and approaches is beneficial for a coach as it will allow her to address topics which may require a change *in thinking* before a sustainable change *in behaviour* can be achieved.

FIND OUT MORE

Essential Psychology: A Concise Introduction (Banyard et al., 2010) is an accessible and clearly written introduction to the field. It covers six areas of psychology that are covered in most university courses. The short, readable chapters will give a reader a foundational understanding, allowing for better decision-making about which areas may require further investigation.

Relationship between thoughts and behaviours

However, using technical language or psychological jargon is hardly ever conducive to a good coaching conversation! There are a number of alternative approaches for helping coachees to reflect on the relationship between their thoughts and their behaviours. In the following section, we will consider some helpful ways of discussing this: the concept of the 'inner game' (Gallwey, 1974), a quote by a Greek philosopher, a thought-provoking series of statements, a Shakespearean passage and a list of 'thinking errors'.

1. The 'inner game'

Gallwey's notion of the 'inner game' was originally introduced in 1974. As a tennis player, and then a tennis coach, Gallwey was interested in the relationship between what happened in the mind of a player and what happened (physically) on the court. In a concept that quickly outgrew the tennis context and then the sports context, Gallwey proposed that 'every game is composed of two parts, an outer game and an inner game' (1974: 11). The outer game is the one that is played on the tennis court, between two players. The inner game 'takes place within the mind of the player and it is played against such obstacles as lapses in concentration, nervousness, self-doubt and self-condemnation. In short, it is played to overcome all habits of mind which inhibit excellence in performance' (1974: 11). Gallwey argued that in order for people to 'maximise their own potential' they must win both the 'outer game' (what happens in the 'real' or external world around us) as well as the 'inner game' (the world of our mind).

What About You?

Many of us experience Gallwey's concept of the 'inner game' regularly when we engage in what is called 'self-talk'. Self-talk describes the 'inner voice' that operates in our mind in certain situations. It is the dialogue that we have with ourselves. For example, in job interview situations, many people experience negative self-talk. This may include thoughts such as 'I am really bad at interviews', 'I haven't got enough experience compared to the other candidates', or 'Why did I even think I would get this job?'. In this case, performance at the job interview is the 'outer game'. This is visible to the interviewers. At the same time, there is another game going on. The second game involves the negative self-talk that the applicant is engaging in. This, obviously, is not directly visible to the interviewers. Gallwey's point, however, is that the 'inner game' influences the 'outer game', and therefore it is important for the player to give attention to the 'inner game'.

Can you think of any self-talk that you have engaged in recently? What impact is it having on your 'outer game'?

Although Gallwey's contribution in 1974 was to significantly impact on the coaching profession, the thoughts that underpin the concept of the 'inner game' can be traced back to classical times.

2. Greek philosopher

In the first century of the Common Era, the Greek philosopher, Epictetus, (55–c.135 CE) is reported by one of his disciples to have said: 'Men are disturbed, not by the things that happen, but by their opinion of the things that happen.' This view suggests two different factors: things that happen (the 'outer game') and a person's opinion of those things (the 'inner game').

3. Thought-provoking Kantian koan

The following thought-provoking series of statements ('old Kantian koan') has been attributed to the philosopher, Immanuel Kant (Peltier, 2010).

> I see a tiger
> I think I am in danger
> I feel afraid
> I run away

Activity   Take a moment to reflect deeply on this series of statements. How do they relate to the concept of the 'inner game'?

This series of statements provides us with an interesting way of thinking about how human behaviour may occur. 'I see a tiger' could be termed an 'activating event'. This is something that we can observe or hear. This event triggers a thought ('I think I am in danger'). The thought then leads to a feeling (in this case, fear). The feeling causes us to behave in a certain way (in this case, running away).

What is powerful for us as coaches is the chance of helping others to recognise that there are stages within this process that are easier for them to control than others. Sometimes we cannot control the activating event, and often we assume that it is the activating event that leads directly to the behaviour (based on the stimulus–response theory of behavioural psychology). It is empowering for a coachee to recognise that if she is able to change the way she thinks about an activating event, it will lead to a different set of feelings.

Please remember that this is simply a way of understanding the process that may be helpful in a coaching conversation, rather than a scientifically proven theory. Despite the recent surge of interest and research into neuroscience, we are still at a very early stage of understanding what happens within the human mind.

FIND OUT MORE

Neuropsychology for Coaches: Understanding the Basics (Brown and Brown, 2012) provides a good introduction to this rapidly developing area.

Story from Practice

Fortunately for many of us, the chance of encountering an unsupervised tiger in our everyday lives is remote. However, the series of four statements discussed above can help us to reflect on our thought processes. The case below is based on a piece of consultancy work that I undertook for a large public sector organisation.

As part of a contract which involved one-to-one executive coaching, I was asked to support a group of middle managers in a large organisation undergoing significant change. In order to get to know the client and get a sense of the proposed changes, I asked to attend an 'away-day' to hear a presentation by the chief executive. The four people I would be coaching were in attendance, along with most of the organisation's middle and senior managers. The coaching was scheduled to take place relatively soon after the presentation, so I introduced myself to each of my coachees, but sat by myself so that I could concentrate on the chief executive's presentation.

The chief executive started by saying how proud she was to lead the organisation and why she had chosen to work for it. She followed with a seemingly honest appraisal of the challenges that lay ahead, suggesting that there would be difficulties and explicitly stating that the organisation would have to shed jobs in order to survive over the coming years. The

(Continued)

(Continued)

chief executive praised the work of the change management team. I was pleased that she mentioned the important role of coaching to support key members of the team through the change process. She concluded by asserting her confidence in the organisation's people and her belief that implementing the required changes would ultimately lead to a more vibrant and effective organisation. In total, she spoke for about 30 minutes. There was some muted applause after which the chief executive left. The away-day continued in her absence. I also left at the same time, and then met with all the executives for a coaching session within two weeks of the away-day.

At the coaching sessions, I chose to ask each client about her or his view of the presentation by the chief executive. At the time, my reason for this was that it seemed to be a good starting point for the discussion and it was also the only experience that I had in common with the coachees. I was genuinely surprised by the significant discrepancy of individual perceptions with relation to the presentation. Considering this using the series of statements above, the chief executive's input was the 'tiger'. During the coaching, each coachee presented me with her or his thoughts and feelings about the presentation. All four were different (although they all experienced exactly the same event). One coachee had a very positive impression. She told me that she was impressed with the leadership qualities of the chief executive. The coachee admired the 'honesty and integrity' of the chief executive as well as her ability to 'face up to reality'. The previous chief executive had always 'worn rose-tinted spectacles' and avoided confrontation. According to this coachee, this was one of the reasons that the organisation was facing such challenges now. The presentation had left her more motivated and committed to supporting the chief executive through the change programme, especially as the hard work of the middle managers had been recognised.

When I spoke to Client 2, it was as if he had attended a different presentation! He shared a very negative response, and was reluctant to discuss the topic in detail. He thought the speech was self-serving and cynical. 'I don't need her to tell me that she did me a favour by coming here as chief executive! I've been here long enough to tell you that she's only interested in her own career. She'll be long gone before this thing blows up.' He saw as 'typical' her behaviour of abandoning any real responsibility for the change programme by 'dumping it' on the middle managers of the organisation. He conceded that she was 'honest' about redundancies, but not the scale of job cuts. 'And we all know that already', he said, dismissing the value of the information. Following the speech, he was even more convinced than before that the chief executive was good at giving presentations ('she's good at the PR') but did not really understand the business or the concerns of staff. As usual, *he* would be expected to make the difficult decisions, and, at the end of the day, it was his job and those of his team members that were at risk. He was already a member of the union and said he would be working with them to resist the proposed changes. In his view, attending the away-day had been a waste of time. He would prefer to invest his time in running the business rather than 'navel-gazing'.

You can see from Table 8.1 that the activating event was the same, and that the ultimate behaviours are very different. Using this visual representation, it becomes

Table 8.1 Different responses to the same activating event.

	Client 1	Client 2
'I see a tiger' Activating event	Presentation by Chief Executive	Presentation by Chief Executive
'I think I am in danger' Thoughts (cognition)	• Chief executive is being honest • Chief executive is an effective leader • Chief executive is making the right decisions • Chief executive appreciates the work we're doing	• Presentation is a cynical ploy to prepare staff for redundancies • Chief executive is good at making speeches but does not know the business • Chief executive will be onto her next job soon, and doesn't care about the impact of her decisions • Chief executive is abandoning responsibility by getting middle managers to deal with all the difficult decisions
'I feel afraid' Feelings (emotion)	Reassured, valued, encouraged, motivated	Anger, resentment, disengagement, fear
'I run away' Behaviour	Engaged in away-day planning Emailed chief executive to thank her	Did not engage in away-day Will resist any changes to ways of working Will not attend future away-days

more evident that the intervening stages are significant. In many cases, we are not in control of the various activating events in our lives. However, what is powerful is the concept that we can influence our own responses by adapting our thoughts.

This story may also help to highlight the difficulty (in the case of Client 2) of adopting a behavioural approach that would focus the coaching on 'being more engaged during away-days'. A simplistic use of the GROW process to look at strategies for participanting more positively at future away-days would ignore the underlying thoughts and feelings of anger and resentment. Some would argue that it would be impossible (in this case) to bring about any lasting change *without* addressing the coachee's thoughts and emotions.

4. Shakespearean interlude

William Shakespeare explored the question of how a person's perceptions can 'create' his own reality.

Hamlet: What have you, my good friends, deserv'd at the hands of Fortune, that she sends you to prison hither?
Guildenstern: Prison, my lord?
Hamlet: Denmark's a prison.
Rosencrantz: Then is the world one.

Hamlet:	A goodly one, in which there are many confines, wards, and dungeons, Denmark being one o' th' worst.
Rosencrantz:	We think not so, my lord.
Hamlet:	Why then 'tis none to you; for there is nothing either good or bad, but thinking makes it so. To me it is a prison. (*Hamlet*, 2.2.228–237)

Hamlet's line, 'there is nothing either good or bad, but thinking makes it so' eloquently and simply captures the power of the 'inner game'. Through Hamlet's own thought processes, Denmark *is* a prison. He accepts that the same place (Denmark) may *not* be a prison for Rosencrantz and Guildenstern. As coaches, we must recognise that a coachee's thoughts can create her reality. In other words, Rosencrantz and Guildenstern are unlikely to get anywhere by simply arguing with Hamlet about whether Denmark is a prison or not. There would be more value in understanding how Hamlet has arrived at the conclusion by supporting him to reflect on the thought process itself.

Talking about the 'inner game'

There are a number of ways of making the 'inner game' more explicitly a focus of a coaching conversation.

1. Practical uses of Kant's koan

Firstly, knowing the 'old Kantian koan' (Peltier, 2010) would allow the coach to explore the coachee's process from the 'activating event' through to a behaviour. The coach can simply ask questions that mirror the series of statements:

Activating event

'Tell me more about what happened initially.'
'So, what started this off?'
'What triggered this situation?'

Thoughts

'And what did you think of that?'
'What thoughts sprang to mind when that happened?'
'What was going through your head at that moment?

Feelings

'And how did those thoughts make you feel?'
'Tell me how that kind of thinking made you feel.'
'What sort of emotions were triggered when those thoughts were in your head?'

Behaviour

'So, what did you do?'
'What's the relationship between these feelings and what you did afterwards?'

When using this conversationally, we can encourage coachees to recognise that they *are* able to change the way they perceive certain situations. We can observe that there is usually a link between what we think and how we feel – and that feelings can influence how we behave.

2. Quote from Epictetus or Shakespearean passage

For coachees who may find philosophy or drama engaging, it may be helpful to share the quote from Epictetus or the passage from *Hamlet*, allowing for a discussion about how our perceptions create our realities.

3. Gallwey's 'inner game'

The concept of the 'inner game' can be explained. If the coachee recognises that her topic relates to her 'outer game', she may be more open to talking about the 'inner game' during the coaching conversation. Alternatively, if the topic is about the 'inner game', the coach and coachee can discuss how this affects the 'outer game'.

Thinking errors and common cognitive distortions

The field of psychology has identified a number of cognitive distortions that can impact negatively on our thinking. These 'thinking errors' can affect us at any time but are especially likely during challenging times or when we are feeling stressed. There are many common cognitive distortions. Twenty of the thinking errors that may be helpful to explore during coaching conversations are listed below.

1. Polarised thinking

This refers to 'black and white' thinking. Although life is usually not this clearly delineated, people can fall into the trap of seeing things as opposites. This way of thinking necessarily limits choices. Statements such as 'I **never** win anything' and 'I am **always** the one who ends up apologising' demonstrate polarised thinking.

2. Over-generalising

This refers to making general or exaggerated statements based on limited information. For example, if someone encounters one person in Brussels being an inconsiderate driver, it would be over-generalising to conclude that 'Belgians are terrible drivers'. Or, if a coachee makes a statement about 'motivation levels in the charity sector' based on one job working for a charity shop, this is another example of over-generalising.

3. Catastrophising

Catastrophising occurs when a person focuses unhelpfully on a mistake to such an extent that a relatively small error begins to feel like a catastrophe. People who catastrophise tend to move quickly in their thinking to the 'worst case scenario'.

4. Personalisation

Basically, this is about taking everything personally. If a coachee feels that everyone's actions are directed at her, this will lead to anxiety and defensiveness. People who get caught by this thinking error find it difficult to receive any feedback, as they are likely to take any suggestions as criticism.

5. Blaming

This is a relatively common thinking error involving the coachee blaming others completely for things that go wrong. By doing this, the coachee does not have to acknowledge her role in a problem or difficult situation.

6. Mindreading

This is when we think that we can tell what someone else is thinking, and unreasonably, we believe that this guess is true (in other words, that we 'know' what may be going on in someone else's head).

7. Self-criticism

Some people believe that criticism is a good way of motivating oneself. This can lead to self-critical thoughts, and people can end up holding unreasonably high expectations for themselves. The fallacy is that such a view is actually beneficial. While it can motivate for short periods of time, it is destructive in the longer term.

8. Unchanging feelings

This thinking error involves believing that because we feel a particular way about something, that we will always feel the same way. An example is someone who says 'I won't want to retire in the south of France because I get bored in quiet towns.'

9. Halo effect

This effect occurs when we believe that everything about a person is wonderful just because we have experienced one positive trait.

10. Minimising

This is when we underplay our role in successful events or positive outcomes. People who minimise their achievements would say 'Oh, that was nothing' or 'I didn't do much,' even when they contributed significantly.

11. Self-serving bias

This is when we attribute positive events to one's own behaviour but negative events to external factors.

12. Assumed similarity

This thinking error is based on believing that other people have similar thoughts and attitudes to ours.

13. In-group bias

The in-group bias is a tendency to trust and value people who are like you or from a similar cultural or social background.

14. Positively based predictions

This is a common error, especially in optimists. A positively based prediction is when we assume things will go well without any evidence to support this.

15. Repeating the same behaviour and expecting different results

Some people continue to repeat their behaviour, or do more of the same thing, and hope for a different result. For example, when nagging a child to clean her room doesn't work, we sometimes simply increase the level of nagging!

16. Labelling

This is when we attach labels to a group of people, making assumptions about how that group behave. Examples are 'IT people', 'lawyers', 'management' etc. Labelling people can allow us to dehumanise them. For example, to suggest that 'the management should be taken out and shot' may seem like an acceptable thing to say until we consider that 'the management' is a group of human beings.

17. Dwelling on the negative

This denotes a tendency to focus solely on the negative, even when there is a broad range of information. For example, focusing on one negative comment on a report card when it is generally positive would suggest that we are dwelling on the negative.

18. Emotional reasoning

Emotional reasoning refers to situations when we take our feelings to represent facts. For example, we might believe that if we're feeling awkward, we are being awkward.

19. Fallacy of fairness

This relates to the unfortunately untrue belief that life is fair. This can cause anger or make us feel like victims. For example, if someone with lesser qualifications gets a promotion, this can seem 'unfair', and lead to demotivation or bitterness.

20. Always being right

This is difficult to believe! We are not always right. If you are surprised by how often you are right and everyone else is wrong, take it as a warning sign that you might be dealing with a cognitive error!

Performance inhibiting thoughts

Cognitive distortions or common thinking errors are also referred to as 'performance inhibiting thoughts' (Palmer and Szymanska, 2007). Palmer and Szymanska suggest that the term 'performance inhibiting thoughts' (PITs) is more appropriate for coaching contexts. This is because it focuses on the fact that the thoughts are preventing the coachee from achieving her desired performance.

Practical use in coaching sessions

A coachee can be asked to list her PITs following discussion with the coach. Once the coachee has identified her PITs, the coach can ask powerful questions to check the accuracy of each. Once the PIT has been examined, the coachee is asked to create 'performance enhancing thoughts' (PETs) for each of the PITs. This is a challenging task that can reap significant rewards.

The role of the coach is to ask powerful questions that allow the coachee to examine the PITs. Are they true? What can be done to prevent the PIT from getting in the way of goal attainment?

Some typical questions are:
'What is the evidence for your belief?'
'What is the impact of this way of thinking?'
'How can you create new thoughts that will support you in achieving your goals?'

Conclusion

This chapter has explored how to coach people on their thinking when adapting behaviours may not be sufficient to achieve sustainable change. The GROW model can still be used, but coaches can help coachees to reflect on their thinking processes using some of the approaches and tools mentioned in this chapter. It is important to remember that we should always be guided by the best interests of the coachee. There will be times when the change required is behavioural. In these circumstances, exploring the 'inner game' can be counterproductive. However, there will also be cases when any behavioural changes will be short lived unless a coachee's way of thinking is altered.

9
USING POSITIVE PSYCHOLOGY

Now that we have covered the skills of coaching and one well-known coaching process, let us consider the contribution of positive psychological approaches. In this chapter, we will first consider the solution-focused coaching approach and some helpful techniques. We will then turn our attention to the broader field of positive psychology by looking at ways of integrating certain interventions into our coaching practice.

Solution-focused coaching

Approach and model

The solution-focused approach to coaching can be used as a discrete model or as part of the GROW process. As you will see below, the solution-focused approach can also be adopted as part of our everyday interactions.

The solution-focused coaching approach emerged from a therapeutic intervention developed in the 1960s and 1970s. At the heart of the 'brief therapy' approach were two principles considered radical at the time. Firstly, that the purpose of therapy was not to simply clarify a difficulty or situation but to make it better in some significant way. Secondly, that the therapist should accept whatever the client said, and that this should be used positively. Essentially, this thinking challenged the traditional approach to therapy of the time by suggesting that it was not crucial to understand the history of a problem (which was the preferred method of the psychotherapeutic approach). The new thinking highlighted the importance of focusing very clearly on helping the client to develop new behaviours to resolve the problem instead. In its early phases, the approach was known as 'brief' therapy because it was seen to have a narrower focus. However, it is probably true to say that current interest in this approach is due to the perception that this approach can take less time.

Solution-focused approaches

The original 'solution-focused' model was developed by de Shazer and Berg, who underscored the positive nature of the interaction. For them, the approach was based on two premises: that the future is 'created' and that small changes in the present can lead to big differences in the future (de Shazer and Berg, 1995). Based on this, de Shazer and Berg proposed that the focus on the intervention should rest on only one question: 'How will we know when the problem is solved?'

Using the scaling technique as the process for a coaching conversation

One of the preferred techniques of the solution-focused approach is called 'scaling'. It is possible to manage an entire coaching conversation using this technique, which is described below.

Following an introduction and agreement about the situation for discussion, the coach can draw or provide a scale which has '1' on one end and '10' on the other.

Step 1: The first step is to place the current situation on the scale, using this question (or similar): 'On a scale of 1–10, with 1 being the worst it could be and 10 being when the situation is resolved, where are you today?' By doing this, we are helping the coachee to put the situation in perspective (this counteracts the 'catastrophising' thinking error mentioned in Chapter 8). It is important that the coachee makes a commitment and identifies a point on the scale. If she prefers to choose a whole number or a fraction, that is OK, as long as she makes a physical mark on the scale of where she considers her situation to be at that moment.

Step 2: Once the coachee has made a commitment regarding where her situation is at the moment, the coach should follow it up by asking the coachee why she has placed it where she has, using a question such as 'What makes it a [whatever number they have chosen] and not a '1'? This question is helpful because it starts to help the coachee acknowledge that some things are already going right. It allows the coach to spend time listening for the existing resources of the coachee. The coach's role here is to celebrate any number that is higher than '1' (see story from practice). As with the GROW model, these early steps are an opportunity to demonstrate active listening and empathy.

Step 3: After listening to the coachee explain why she has placed the situation where she did, and celebrating the fact that it is not a '1', the coach moves onto the most important stage of the solution-focused approach. The coach should ask what a '9' or '10' would look like: 'What would it look/feel like if the situation were at a 9 or 10?' We ask this question to encourage the coachee to imagine life without the problem. As a coach, you may want to spend some time talking about this situation, as this is usually very motivational. Ask the coachee to really start to imagine what it would be like if this situation were completely resolved. It is appropriate to spend most of the time allocated for coaching to this step. The positive emotions generated here will provide the motivation for the coachee to tackle the situation effectively.

Step 4: Once the coach senses that the coachee is motivated by the thought of a successful outcome, the following question (or similar) is asked: 'What would make you move the situation to [a slightly higher number than originally chosen]?' In other words, the coach is asking what small steps could be taken to increase the coachee's perception of the situation. So, if the coachee had rated the current situation as a '4', the coach would ask 'And what would need to happen for you to rate it as a '5'? This step will seem relatively manageable, and the coachee should be more able to think of something to move them towards the '5'. The coach's role here is to support the coachee to come up with some very practical and achievable steps that would lead to the coachee placing her situation slightly higher on the scale (and therefore closer to when the situation will be completely resolved). It is crucial that this comes from the coachee, and that a specific action plan is agreed. The important factor is that the coachee starts to feel that she is moving towards the solution. Remember that one of the principles of this approach is that a small change now can lead to a big difference in the future. Additionally, a small step will feel manageable to the coachee, and success in achieving that small step will motivate her further.

The coaching would be concluded at this point, with a date set for the next session. Assuming that the coachee has achieved her small step, the process would be followed again, but this time exploring the next small step. If the coachee does not feel that she has achieved the small step, other ways of moving forward can be discussed.

Story from Practice

The solution-focused coaching process identified here is not always the most appropriate for every coachee. I have selected an example that was particularly suited to this approach. In my experience, this approach works best when there is a clear barrier or difficulty that the coachee is facing. In other words, the need for coaching will have arisen because the coachee is too focused on what is going *wrong* instead of focusing on what is going well.

The coachee, a first line manager in an organisation, wanted to talk about her career development. Up to that point, due to a number of factors including family commitments, this coachee had allowed her career to 'happen to her', without trying to shape it. She felt that she was a hard worker and that this had been duly recognised. She had been promoted internally to her current role, which she had been doing now for six years. She felt ready to move into a more senior role but worried that her low levels of confidence about interviews would let her down, and therefore did not apply for jobs that she saw advertised.

As there seemed to be a clear 'blockage' (something that was evidently getting in the way of the coachee achieving her aspirations), I felt that the solution-focused process would be helpful. I explained that we would be using the 'solution-focused scale' to frame our conversation and produced a sheet of paper with a pre-printed scale. I asked her to reflect on her confidence levels about interviews and place them on the scale, explaining that '10' would denote that she felt incredibly confident about interviews, and that '1' would suggest that she had no confidence at all. After reflecting for about 10 seconds, she said '3' with some uncertainty. I asked her to take a pen and mark the scale at that point. As she was about to do this, she said 'maybe a 4, actually. Can I say 3 and a half?' I replied that she could choose any number that she felt correctly represented her current level of confidence. She settled for a '4'. Once she had made her decision, I noted positively that a '4' is relatively good. I asked her what made her select '4' instead of a '1' or a '2'. Although hesitantly at first, she was able to explain all the reasons that it was a '4': she had been successful at the interview for the current job, she was recently invited to be part of an interview panel for a new member of staff and she felt she would have very good references. Talking about these things seemed to build her confidence, and she became less hesitant as she listed the reasons that she had selected a '4'. I concluded by commenting on the fact that she seemed to have a good foundation to build on. I then moved onto the most important part of the process: 'What would it need to be like for you to rate your confidence as a '9' or a '10'? We spent about 30 minutes of the 1-hour session on this conversation. She became animated as she talked about how she would feel, what type of preparation she would have completed and how she would know each of the members of the interview panel. Most of her ideas related to feeling confident because she would be well-prepared, aware of what questions to expect and knowing the members of the interview panel. As she was talking, she realised that if she applied for a job internally, it was very likely that she *would* know everyone on the panel. Moving into the final stage, I asked the coachee what she could do *now* or in the near future to get her own rating of her confidence about interviews from a '4' to a '5'. Based on her assertion that 'being more prepared' would help her to feel more confident, she said that she would rate her confidence at a '5' if she had a completed, up-to-date CV and notes about some of her professional successes over the last six years. As she reflected on this, she said 'actually, if I do these things, it'll probably be a 6'. She agreed to do both these things before the next session.

Solution-focused coaching techniques

There are a number of solution-focused coaching techniques that can be used within other coaching processes, such as GROW.

Scaling

The first is the scaling approach described above. While it can be used as a stand-alone framework for a coaching conversation, it can also feature as part of the GROW process. For example, it can be very helpful in the 'will' or 'way forward' stage. A good question to ask is: 'How committed are you to the actions you've just chosen on a scale from 1 to 10?' Then the process above can be used briefly to see whether the level of commitment can be increased in some way.

Exceptions to the problem

In solution-focused coaching, the coach uses the techniques below to support coachees to move quickly towards solutions rather than getting bogged down in the 'current reality' or the 'problem'. Throughout a coaching process, it is helpful for the coach to keep the focus and attention on how the coachee will know when the problem is resolved. That is why it can be helpful to ask questions which aim to find exceptions to problems. So, if a coachee raises a recurring problem or difficulty, the coach can ask the following questions (for example):

- 'Always?'
- 'Are there times when this does not happen?'
- 'Can you think of a time when you were surprised by a different outcome?'

The coach can help the coachee by asking her to identify examples of when the problem does not seem to occur. Time, effort and energy can then be invested into understanding the circumstances for when the problem did not occur, in order to make the exceptions more frequent.

Asking the 'miracle question'

Another way of helping a coachee to focus on a positive future is to ask her what has become known as the 'miracle question'. The wording of the question can be changed, and here is one example of it:

> 'If a miracle happened tonight while you were sleeping and this problem completely disappeared, how would you know tomorrow morning that the miracle had happened?'

In other words, the scenario is that something magical has happened during the night, meaning that the problem has been resolved or no longer exists. However, the coachee does not know that this has occurred during the night. The focus of the conversation should be on how the coachee would find out that the problem is no longer there. The miracle question can be supplemented by asking the coachee what it would be like the following day:

- 'How would others behave?'
- 'How would you be behaving?'
- 'How would you be feeling?'
- 'What would be different at work?'

The reason for this is to encourage the coachee to start talking about life without the problem so that she can turn her attention to the solution (rather than the problem) and see the benefits of making the necessary changes.

Take a moment to watch Video 9.2 'Coach asks coachee to imagine that her fairy godmother had solved the situation'.

SNAPSHOT   Being solution-focused all the time

A solution-focused approach can be helpful in a standalone capacity or as part of your coaching practice. There are many principles of the solution-focused approach that can be incorporated into your coaching as well as everyday life. Here are some of the principles and practices that can be used in everyday life, so that we can be 'solution-focused' all the time.

1. Acknowledge the difficulties that people are facing but do not prolong negative conversations unnecessarily.

2. Minimise talk about the 'causes' of problems when speaking with colleagues or friends.
3. Be curious about what people are doing to manage challenging situations.
4. Avoid asking 'why is this happening?' when people complain about something.
5. Challenge thinking errors when you hear them.
6. Be generous with positive feedback about the successes of others.
7. Encourage others to identify small changes that can start to make a difference in their lives.

A balanced view

After having presented the solution-focused approach so positively above, it is appropriate to also make reference to some of the criticisms that it faces. Some argue that the solution-focused approach can feel forced and move people too quickly towards solutions without acknowledging the difficulties that they are facing. Others predict that any behavioural improvements will be short-lived because the approach seems to ignore any underlying issues. Finally, some people complain that, despite its title, the solution-focused approach is essentially a problem-solving tool, continuing to consider the 'problem' the basis for discussion. In other words, although the discussion is about a 'solution', there is an implied 'problem' somewhere in the background. This last point is a fair challenge, and readers wishing to delve deeper into this debate may want to learn about appreciative coaching which focuses solely on positives.

FIND OUT MORE

There are many books written about appreciative enquiry which you may wish to consult. For a book that focuses specifically on appreciative coaching, the title below is recommended.
   Orem, S.L., Binkert, J. and Clancy, A.L. (2007) *Appreciative Coaching: A Positive Process for Change.* San Francisco, CA: Jossey-Bass.

Using positive psychology when coaching

Positive psychology is a relatively recent subfield of psychology that focuses attention on what is positive about human beings (rather than their deficits). Its interest in 'what makes individuals and communities flourish, rather than languish' (Hefferon and Boniwell, 2011: 2) complements the purpose of coaching. According Dr Carol Kauffman, 'the mission of positive psychology is to develop sound theories of optimal functioning and to find empirically supported ways to improve the lives of ordinary and extraordinary people' (2006: 219). In this section, we will consider the contribution of positive psychology to coaching.

Looking for strengths in others

I have said elsewhere in this book that the role of the coach is that of a strengths-finder. This principle from positive psychology can be understood as a general inclination of the coach. This means that a coach would be listening for strengths throughout a coaching conversation, especially in the earlier stages ('Goal' and 'Reality'). Doing this is helpful in building rapport and increasing the positivity and self-confidence of the coachee. For example, if a coachee is talking about how she dislikes her organisation and complains that she has been there for 15 years, it is possible to note how patient and determined she must have been to remain in an organisation that she did not like for that period of time.

Completing the VIA survey

Another way of using positive psychology in coaching is to invite coachees to complete the VIA Survey of Character Strengths. To access this survey, visit our Companion Website for a link (**www.sagepub.co.uk/vannieuwerburgh**). Coachees will need to answer 240 questions, so this needs to be assigned for completion prior to a coaching session or as an inter-sessional task in between coaching conversations. The VIA Survey of Character Strengths lists a person's top strengths, providing a brief description of each. This allows a coachee's strengths to be the focus of a coaching conversation, with the purpose of the discussion to see what resources the coachee already has, and how she can use existing strengths in more areas of her life.

Using strengths cards

If coaches would prefer to complete this task during the coaching conversation, it is possible to purchase 'strengths cards' which are based on the VIA Survey of Character Strengths. Each strength is presented on a card, allowing the coachee to read about each in more detail. Through the use of the cards, it is possible for the coachee to identify a set of three or five top strengths. This is a very positive and interactive way of talking about strengths that involves both coach and coachee. To find out how to purchase the cards, visit our Companion Website (**www.sagepub.co.uk/vannieuwerburgh**).

Other positive psychological interventions (PPIs)

Positive psychology is an area that is currently flourishing. As it continues to grow its evidence base, new interventions are being proposed. The ones suggested below are only a few of an increasingly broad range of choices, and particularly useful in the context of coaching conversations.

Three good things

This is a simple and effective positive psychological intervention that has been shown to have a beneficial impact on a person's subjective well-being. There are variations but in essence, it involves noting three positive things that happened during the day. Usually, this task is completed in the evening. The positive effect comes from taking time and intentionally reflecting on *what went well* rather than just remembering the things that did not go so well.

Positive reflections journal   Activity

Reflect for a few minutes. Do you have a tendency to prioritise thinking about the things that did not go so well during the day? If so, this activity will help. Use a paper or electronic notebook to create a 'positive reflections' journal. At the end of each day, just note three things that happened which were positive. Then note what you did to make those things happen. Try it for a few weeks. If it works for you, continue to use it. If not, at least you'll have a notebook of positive occurrences that you can look back at in future!

Despite its simplicity, there is research evidence that this method works (Hefferon and Boniwell, 2011). One way of incorporating it into coaching sessions is to ask coachees to reflect on this every time you meet. The straightforward question, 'can you tell me about three good things that have happened since we last met?' necessarily focuses attention on positive occurrences. This can lighten the mood and increase the coachee's enthusiasm. Another way of using this PPI is to ask the coachee to write down three good things about a situation that does not seem positive at all. This can be challenging, but useful. In effect, this PPI counterbalances one of the thinking errors we saw in the previous chapter (dwelling on the negative). If coachees find the activity useful, this PPI can be shared with them and can be used in the way described above (positive reflections journal).

Gratitude letter

This PPI can be shared with the coachee for her to use with people to whom she is grateful. Often in our busy lives, we have little time to properly acknowledge or thank people around us. In some cultures, there is some awkwardness associated with simply telling someone how much you appreciate them. However, there is empirical data that doing so can have a positive affect on both parties (Hefferon and Boniwell, 2011).

The PPI involves writing a letter or email that describes what a person has done for you and the positive impacts that resulted. The purpose is to express genuine gratitude, highlighting how much you appreciate the other person and the things she does. The intervention suggests that the writer should then take the letter to the person (if this is possible) and read it to her. In coaching, this intervention can be explained to the coachee. If appropriate and helpful, the coachee can start to draft the gratitude letter during the coaching session. This intervention can be effective when there has been a disagreement or a 'falling out' between the coachee and someone with whom she has a strong relationship.

What About You?

If you're cringing at the thought of reading such a letter to someone to whom you are genuinely grateful, it's likely that you (and the other party) are likely to get the most out of this activity. How will you summon the courage to do it?

Story from Practice

Having spoken to both writers and recipients of gratitude letters, I know what a powerful experience this can be. I was coaching a newly qualified teacher who had just starting working for the secondary school that he had attended. He was doing a great job in school and seemed to connect with students. The coaching topic related to his interactions with staff in the school, which I won't talk about here. However, during the conversation, the coachee spoke about the fact that he was inspired to become an educator because of an outstanding history teacher who still worked in the school. One of the challenges was the awkwardness of calling this person by his first name, having become so used to speaking to him more formally.

I shared the idea of the gratitude letter with the coachee and asked if he would be interested in drafting it during the coaching session. I could sense the positive emotion in the room as this was happening. In between coaching sessions, the coachee took the letter to his colleague and used this as an aide-memoire while talking to his former teacher at a local cafe. There were tears both at that event and in the telling of it in the coaching session. It strengthened the bond between the two people, acknowledging the gratitude and the positive impact of the older colleague's actions. But it also allowed both of them to acknowledge that there was now a different, professional relationship which could build on this.

In the coaching session, the coachee was very enthusiastic about the exercise and was keen to write gratitude letters to a number of other people. The greatest realisation was that the coachee had assumed that important people in his life somehow knew what he was thinking and how much he appreciated what they did for him. The power of having a face-to-face discussion about this was a revelation. He also acknowledged that doing this had made him feel better about his relationships with other colleagues in the school.

Best possible self

This PPI involves thinking and writing about yourself imagining that you have achieved everything you want for yourself. This should be done regularly and consistently over the period of a month so that there is continuous and recurring opportunity to imagine yourself in this desired future state. The benefits can be immediate (feeling better about yourself) but can also be helpful for coaching because the coachee will have a clearer image about what she is working towards, and this is motivational. Again, this activity can be started during a coaching conversation.

Conclusion

In this chapter, we have taken time to build on the GROW process by exploring how solution-focused approaches and positive psychological interventions may enhance our practice. As we will discuss in Chapters 14 and 15, these approaches may also inform the necessary 'way of being' for coaches. As Hefferon and Boniwell (2011) point out 'coaching and positive psychology are natural allies in sharing an explicit concern with the enhancement of optimal functioning and wellbeing, arguing for performance improvement, finding what is right with the person and working on enhancing it' (p. 209).

FIND OUT MORE

The best and most accessible short text on positive psychology is Ilona Boniwell's *Positive Psychology in a Nutshell* (2012). It does what it says on the cover!

PART FOUR

PRACTICAL TOOLS AND TECHNIQUES

10
BODY LANGUAGE AND EMOTIONAL INTELLIGENCE

Human beings are social animals. We like to communicate with one another, and do so in a number of different ways. We often focus on speaking or writing when we think about how people communicate. However, we also communicate through intentional and unintentional body language.

The role of body language in coaching

Body language is an important consideration for coaches. We will explore this from two perspectives: noticing the body language of our coachees and being aware of the messages that we may be sending back through our own body language.

We have already shown that the coach has many responsibilities during a coaching conversation. The coach should be listening actively, asking powerful questions, summarising and paraphrasing, giving and receiving feedback, managing the coaching process and employing a range of positive psychological and solution focused approaches. In addition, it is also helpful for the coach to be alert for information and collect interesting data. In a coaching conversation, data is everywhere. This includes what is spoken (and not), what happens between the coach and the coachee, what each party is wearing, what each is thinking or feeling, among many other factors. Body language is a rich source of information for a coach.

A coachee's body language can provide the coach with useful information before, during, and after a coaching conversation. As coaches, we should avoid being too confident about what certain types of body language indicate. Body language provides *supplementary* data which may give the coach clues about what the coachee may be feeling or thinking. Such data should be used with caution, and only in conjunction with questions to ensure that inaccurate assumptions are not made.

Tables 10.1, 10.2 and 10.3 list some commonly seen gestures and body postures with an indication of what each *may* suggest. These are not scientifically proven or verifiable.

As the coaching conversation progresses, the coach can be alert for changes to body language and notice the level of engagement or discomfort of the coachee. This is partly to ensure that appropriate questions are asked, but also so that any observations can be fed back to the coachee.

Table 10.1   Body language clues: posture

Body Posture	Possible Meanings
Leaning forward	Anticipation, excitement Engaged in topic Eagerness to leave
Leaning backward	Comfortable Does not want to talk about topic being discussed Repulsed, disgusted
Standing upright	Reserved Confident Formal
Stooped shoulders	Dejected Deflated Feeling hopeless

Table 10.2   Body language clues: hands

Hands	Possible Meanings
Fists clenched	Nervous Angry
Drumming fingers	Irritated Impatient
Hands clasped	Comfortable Wishing for something
Hands in steeple shape	Feeling superior Thinking deeply
Biting fingernails	Anxious Impatient
Hand on chin	Thinking
Rubbing chin	Thinking Evaluating
Hand in front of mouth	Concealing something Does not believe what she has just said
Finger in front of mouth	Thinks that she should not speak Thinks of something that should not be discussed
Head leaning on hand	Bored Demotivated
Hand on forehead	Worried Embarrassed or ashamed
Finger on temple	Instructing self to think

Hands	Possible Meanings
Scratching head	Instructing self to think Embarrassed
Touching nose	Has said something she does not believe
Stroking head	Self-comforting Rewarding self
Playing with hair	Self-comforting
Touching eyebrows	Trying to hide Embarrassed
Playing with fringe	Trying to hide Embarrassed
Clutching armrest of chair	Fear
Rubbing hands together	Anticipation Savouring a future moment

Table 10.3   Body language clues: arms and legs

Arms	Possible meanings
Crossed	Defensive Feeling protective about topic
Linked behind head	Feeling superior Aggressive
Dangling behind chair	Disengaged
Stroking shoulder	Self-comforting Rewarding self
Stroking forearms	Self-comforting

Legs	Possible meanings
Crossed	Defensive Uncomfortable about topic
Feet twisted around each other	Anxious Uncomfortable about topic
Stroking thighs	Self-comforting
Feet swinging	Playful Feeling dependent
Legs bouncing up and down	Anxious Impatient
Legs stretched out to the front	Feeling comfortable

FIND OUT MORE

One of the best books on the topic is *The Definitive Book of Body Language* (Pease and Pease, 2005).

Facial expressions

The facial expressions of both the coachee and the coach may provide further information about what may be happening beneath the surface. Facial expressions can provide a link to the 'inner game' of the coachee. Even when people attempt to hide their true thoughts and feelings, it is possible to pick up 'micro expressions' which are almost impossible to suppress.

FIND OUT MORE

If you are interested in studying facial expressions, Professor Paul Ekman is the world's leading authority in this area. To start your exploration, visit the Companion Website for a link to his online materials (**www.sagepub.co.uk/vannieuwerburgh**).

How to use body language in coaching

As stated previously, body language can only provide us with hints or additional information. Coaches must be careful not to draw inappropriate conclusions based on body language alone. For example, it has been suggested that touching one's nose may suggest that someone is lying. Equally, the coachee might have an itchy nose.

A very effective use of body language is to reflect certain aspects of this back to the coachee. Often coachees are not aware of their own body language, and therefore may benefit from having this information. For example, a coach could notice that a coachee is much more animated when talking about one of her options. In this case, the coach could say 'When you were talking about the idea of setting up your own business, you sat forward and spoke more quickly. Did you notice that?' An opposite example would be if a coachee said that she was excited about a certain course of action and her body language did not convey the same impression. A coach could challenge the coachee by saying 'You've said that you are committed to this course of action, even using the word "excited", but I noticed that you were sitting back in your chair and not very animated when you were describing it.'

The coachee's body language can also be used to inform the way in which the coach manages the session. You may, for example, want to take notes about certain examples of positive or negative body language in order to return to particular topics later, or avoid them. For example, if talking about communication within her organisational team seems to completely demotivate the coachee, it may be preferable at times to avoid the topic. Conversely, if you have noted that talking about promotion seems to give the coachee energy, you may want to bring this up just before the end of the session.

Watching people   Activity

This activity will take an hour of your time, but may also pass as a pleasant coffee break. Go to a cafe on your own, with a notebook or tablet device. Once you've ordered your drink, sit at a table and watch the people around you. Try to do this discreetly! Look for the body language signals mentioned in this chapter, jotting them down when you see them. Next to each make some notes about what information is provided by the body language that you've noticed. If you're in Paris when you do this, you don't need to be discreet about it. People-watching is a national pastime!

Cultural specificity

If you need a good excuse for a holiday, try to convince yourself that you need to go on a short break to somewhere which has a different culture so that you can observe differences with body language.

There is no doubt that the extent to which we use our bodies to express our thoughts and feelings varies depending on many social and cultural factors. As coaches, we need to be careful to be sensitive to cultural differences. People from some cultures use their hands much more when talking than others. This does not necessarily mean that they are unusually excited about what they are talking about. Equally when people in some cultures speak loudly to one another, we must not assume that they are being aggressive. Eye contact also varies significantly between cultures. It is appropriate in some cultures to maintain eye contact for relatively long periods of time, while in others eye contact should be brief or even avoided. Such avoidance should not necessarily be taken to suggest shyness.

Coach's body language

The first part of this chapter has looked at the body language of the coachee. Let us now turn our attention to the body language of the coach. Initially, coaches must become aware of their own body language. What messages does your body give out, and what, if anything, is your face saying without your permission? As coaches, our communications are at the heart of the coaching process. Each question, each time we summarise, each silence and each nod has significance. For this reason, coaches need to manage all forms of communication with their coachees. We should avoid discrepancies between what we say verbally and the messages we give through our facial expressions or body language.

Remember that your coachee may also be the proud owner of this book, and may also have access to this chapter which lists various body language signals. They may be interpreting your every move! For this reason, it is helpful to develop a fairly neutral stance for use during coaching conversations. Open body language is helpful when creating relationships or listening actively. When you are learning to coach, it is natural to feel a bit nervous, but it is better to minimise the visual signs of anxiety. For example, make sure that you are not fidgeting, playing with a pen or biting your fingernails. This kind of anxious behaviour is contagious, and it can affect the coachee's level of comfort with the session. See an example of appropriate body language by watching Video 10.2.

Matching and mismatching

As one of two people in the coaching room, what you do has a profound impact on the session. Of course, the same applies the other way round – what the coachee does has a profound impact on the session too. However, it is the coach who is managing the process and supporting the coachee to find ways to achieve more of her potential. To aid with this, it is useful to occasionally be intentional about our use of body language.

During the early stages of the coaching conversation, it is important to match your body language to that of the coachee. This is one of the ways that human beings build rapport. The more that the person we are talking to behaves like we do, the more comfortable we are, and the stronger the relationship. So, for example, if the coachee has her arms crossed, the coach may choose to do the same. Or if the coachee is leaning forward when speaking, the coach can lean in too. Novice coaches often worry that this will be too obvious. Of course, it is helpful to do this discreetly, but this actually happens naturally when two people are connected well to one another. So, a coachee is unlikely to feel that there is something strange going on if both of you have your arms crossed.

Matching is useful in the early stages, especially in the Reality stage when the coach is most likely to do the most listening. Loosely matching the coachee's body language will allow her to feel more relaxed and listened to. Take time to notice how the body language changes based on what the coachee is talking about. By consciously being aware of body language, the coach will be better able to gather important data about what irritates the coachee, motivates her or bores her. See Video 10.3 'Coach and coachee having matched body lanuage'.

The intentional use of body language in coaching also includes *mismatching*. While the primary concern in the first two stages of the GROW model is to build rapport and strengthen the relationship, the final two stages should be about passing responsibility onto the coachee and helping her to be motivated about what she is going to do. For this reason, it may be helpful at times to mismatch body language. If the coachee seems demotivated and lacking in energy during the Options phase, it may be helpful to introduce some liveliness into the coaching session by using more hand gestures, leaning forward, or speaking more loudly. Because of the early mirroring, the coachee is likely to follow the coach's lead and become more lively. However, sometimes the reverse may be the case. If the coachee is very excitable, jumping from one possibility to another during the latter stages of a coaching conversation, it may help to bring energy levels down by speaking more slowly, putting your hands in your lap and sitting back slightly, allowing for more silences during the conversation. Again, if handled well, this will slow the pace of the conversation and allow the coachee to consider her options in a more measured way.

Film yourself coaching   Activity

One of the best ways of enhancing your coaching practice is to film yourself coaching others. If this is a daunting prospect, all the more reason for doing it. All you need is a video camera and a willing coachee!

When filming a coaching session, be aware that you may need a bit longer than usual to get relaxed, so perhaps spend a bit more time on small talk. Once you get into the coaching, it is sometimes possible to forget that the camera is there.

It may be helpful to start by filming a 20–30 minute coaching session. For the purposes of a practice session, it is helpful to follow the GROW process. The coachee should be asked to bring a *real* topic to the session.

When you have finished the session, make a note of what you think you did particularly well. It is not helpful to watch the video straight away. When you do watch the video again, start by looking for evidence of your strengths (what you thought you did really well). Add any comments to your original notes. When watching the video for a second time, stop to think about alternatives to the questions you asked or tools you used. How might you have done things differently?

Finally, watch the video for a third time. This time watch it with no sound. Observe only the body language (both your body language and the coachee's body language). What do you notice? Who was working harder? How similar is the body language? What differences are there?

Emotional intelligence

Another source of information comes from our emotions and those of the coachee. For this reason, coaches should have relatively high levels of emotional intelligence. Only a very brief definition of emotional intelligence will be provided here. Readers who are interested in further enhancing their understanding of the concept are invited to follow this up by selecting one of the recommended texts noted below.

FIND OUT MORE

Daniel Goleman is the person most associated with the concept of emotional intelligence. He popularised the phrase 'emotional intelligence' and his books remain the most accessible and informative on the subject (Goleman, 1996).

The leading writers on the topic of emotional intelligence are John Mayer and Peter Salovey (who developed the concept) and Daniel Goleman (who adapted and popularised it). Salovey and Mayer defined emotional intelligence as 'the ability to monitor one's own and others' feelings and emotions, to discriminate among them and to use this information to guide one's thinking and actions' (1990: 189). For the purposes of coaching, it can be understood as the ability to understand our own feelings, notice the emotions of others, and, importantly, change our behaviour based on this information. Emotional intelligence is not *simply* being able to understand our own feelings and those of other people. Unless we change our behaviour as a result of this understanding, we cannot be said to operate in an emotionally intelligent way.

Tears

Tears should not be avoided in the coaching space. Both coach and coachee are human beings who have emotions. Strong emotions are acceptable in coaching conversations. If you, as the coach, have created the right conditions, the coaching space will feel like a place where it is OK to cry. Tears can signify trust, relief, pain and sadness (amongst other human emotions). For most coaches, the challenge comes not from the fact that the coachee is crying, but because the coach feels awkward and does not know what to do. As always, our focus must be on the coachee and her best interests. If the coachee has chosen to show her true emotions by crying, this is a good thing. It is an indication that you are probably talking about the *right* thing. Every coach will develop her own way of managing tears in the coaching space. In the story from practice below, I have provided some of the techniques that I use, not as a guide but so that you can feel more prepared for tears.

> **Story from Practice**
>
> I always provide tissues during every coaching conversation (not just when I think the coachee is likely to cry during a session!).
>
> If a coachee looks like she is on the verge of tears, I ask whether she would like to carry on with the conversation. This gives the coachee an important set of choices. Some continue, knowing the tears will come. Some want to compose themselves and try to control the tears. Some will stop the conversation and talk about something else. Some will leave the room. Every one of these choices should be made to feel legitimate and welcome in the coaching relationship.
>
> When the coachee is crying, I give time and space for this. I do not apply pressure by asking if the coachee is 'OK'. I do not promise that 'things will be alright'. I do not extend a hand or give the coachee a hug. I do not cry with the coachee. All I do is create a quiet, respectful space where crying is OK.
>
> When the emotions seem to have subsided, I give the responsibility of restarting the session (or not) to the coachee by saying 'Just let me know when and if you'd like to continue with our coaching conversation.'

Conclusion

In this chapter we have considered the important roles of body language and emotional intelligence during coaching conversations. Coaches can enhance their effectiveness by becoming aware of their own body language while monitoring the body language of their coachees. At the same time, coaches need to notice their own emotions and the emotions of the coachee, ensuring that the coach's behaviours respond appropriately and empathically to those of the coachee.

11
INSPIRING CREATIVITY: LET'S TALK

This section covers the use of activities and tools during coaching conversations. Experienced coaches and satisfied coachees often highlight this type of activity as a source of key turning points during coaching conversations. It could be said that the use of such activities differentiates coaching from a number of other one-to-one conversational interventions.

Creativity is required during coaching sessions, especially during the Options stage of the GROW process. In a sense, the Options stage is where new ideas are generated. Novel thinking is required, and many people seek coaching in order to be supported as they explore creative solutions and innovative ways forward. Over three chapters, we will look at ways of inspiring creativity during coaching sessions through conversational techniques, pen-and-paper tasks and active participation.

One- or two-hour coaching sessions can be made more engaging by asking the coachee to complete some conversational, drawing or active tasks. It is useful for the coach to have a toolkit of resources to support these activities. The toolkit should contain high-quality coloured paper, post-it notes, colour pens, pencils and highlighters.

Each of these activities can be adapted to suit the needs of the coach and the coachee. There is no 'correct way' of using these activities and coaches will have to check with coachees about the appropriateness of interventions. Coaches may feel that they are taking a risk by introducing some of these activities, but in the worst case, it is easy enough to change activities. There is nothing wrong with abandoning an activity if it is not meeting the needs of the coachee.

Coaching is appropriately understood as a conversational intervention. As a result, it is to be expected that many people assume that talking is all that happens within a coaching conversation. So, in one way, the activities covered in this chapter can be thought of as 'conventional'. However, my own experience and that of other coaches and former students is that they can sometimes be the key to unlocking a person's potential, the trigger for 'A-ha!' moments and a way to encourage coachees to see things differently. Your own creativity is the limit for conversation-based activities. Below are a few to get you started!

Want to see what these activities look like in practice? You can see all the activities in Chapters 11, 12, and 13 explained by watching the corresponding videos.

Three wishes

Resources

- Picture of a 'magic lamp' or 'genie'
- Or (even better) an old lamp
- Post-it notes
- Pen

Activity

Take out the old lamp (or an image of it) and ask your coachee to imagine that a genie has offered her three wishes relating to the current situation. What would she ask for? At this stage, coachees often seek clarification: 'Any wish?' or 'Do the wishes need to be realistic?' The purpose of the activity is to generate thoughts which are not restricted by what is perceived to be 'realistic', so the coachee should be encouraged to set aside any conceptions about what is or what is not possible for this activity. The only constraints are that there are only three wishes and that these should relate to the topic of the coaching conversation.

As the wishes are chosen, ask the coachee to make a note of these on post-it notes. Once the three wishes have been identified, coach and coachee should move onto the evaluation stage. The coachee is asked to evaluate two things. Firstly, to what extent are some elements of each wish already in place? Secondly, to what extent is it possible to plan some initial steps to move closer to at least one of the wishes?

When it can be helpful

This activity works particularly well in the following situations:

- When the coachee cannot identify positive goals during the Goal stage. In other words, if the coachee can only identify what she wants to avoid. For example, 'I know that I cannot work within this department any more.'
- When the coachee says that she is unable to formulate any further ideas in the Options stage.

Crystal ball

Resources

- Image of a crystal ball
- Or (even better) a crystal ball

Activity

Show the coachee the crystal ball, inviting her to attempt to see into her own future. This may be a very short activity, depending on the openness of the coachee to this type of activity. For this activity to work best, the coachee should be asked to carry the crystal ball. The question to ask is: 'If you look into the crystal ball, and imagine that you can see elements of your future, what are they?' Encourage her to say what she thinks she sees, even if it is 'fuzzy'. Do not push the coachee to be specific. The intention is to discover what the coachee *wants* to see in her future. Analysis and evaluation is not part of this activity. Depending on the outcome of this activity, it may be easier to identify some goals and subgoals relating to the glimpses that the coachee has seen in her future.

When it can be helpful

This activity is helpful during the Goal stage, especially if the coachee is not clear about her goals.

Practical tip

If the coachee is finding it difficult to 'see' anything in the crystal ball, a useful follow-up question can be 'what would you *like* to see in your future?'

11.3 If you did know the answer

Resources

- None

Activity

If we, as coaches, create the right thinking environment, coachees often start to ask seemingly rhetorical questions while they are talking (e.g. 'I know what I want to achieve, but I don't know how others would react to these changes. Will they support me, or are they going to dislike the choices I have made?'). Each rhetorical question posed by the coachee provides an opportunity for the coach. The question is often a probing one, demonstrating that the coachee is starting to reflect more deeply about her situation. At this point, coaches can ask 'And what is the answer to that question?' or 'I'm guessing that you don't know the answer to that question right now, but what do you *think* it might be?' This may lead to further exploration, or a more defensive 'I don't know the answer.' Although this may seem irritating, it is worth pursuing by asking, 'If you *did* know the answer, what would it be?' This question can lead to surprising insights.

When it can be helpful

This can be used at any point during a coaching conversation. It works best when the coachee asks a seemingly rhetorical question of herself.

Random word selection

Resources

- Children's illustrated dictionary

Activity

Place the illustrated dictionary in front of the coachee, asking her to pick a page at random and select the word she finds most interesting or relevant. When she has selected a word, the coachee should be asked to talk for about five minutes about her situation, using that word. Due to the fact that the coachee must approach her topic from a completely new, randomly-selected angle, it can sometimes lead to a helpful insight.

When it can be helpful

This activity is most useful when the coaching session feels 'stuck' and a new way of approaching the topic is required. It is recommended for use in the Reality or Options stages.

Random object

Resources

- Fabric bag containing a number of small objects

Activity

This is a variant of the activity above. Rather than selecting a word at random, the coachee is asked to put a hand into the bag to pick out an object. Capture any initial thoughts about the chosen object. Once she has considered the object, the coachee should be asked how the object could be used to discuss her topic. Present this as a challenge. For example, 'Is there any way that you can bring this object into your discussion about the current situation?'

When it can be helpful

This activity is most useful when the coaching session feels 'stuck' and a new way of approaching the topic is required.

Story from Practice

During the third coaching session, we felt stuck. The goal had been identified in the first session, and some ways forward decided. In the second session, we had focused on progress and the question of how motivated the coachee was to make the changes. We talked about whether the self-selected goal of the coachee was important enough for him to invest significant energy towards making it happen. The coachee came to the third session frustrated. He had not been able to carry out the tasks that he had identified for himself at the previous session. 'I don't know why I cannot stick to some simple commitments that I made to myself. I could make excuses, but in reality, I should have been able to do this!' We decided to explore what was stopping him from delivering on commitments that he made to himself. During the conversation, he concluded that he liked to 'procrastinate', putting off difficult tasks and uncomfortable conversations for as long as possible. He realised that this was a pattern that kept repeating itself. And what frustrated him the most was that he could tell that he was doing it again in relation to the coaching. In this situation, he *knew* that 'procrastination' was something he wanted to address, but the risk was that he would put off tackling this issue because it was difficult to change.

At this point, I asked how the coachee would feel about engaging in a creative activity. With his agreement, I produced a small black bag containing a few items. The coachee became more animated immediately, and put his hand in the bag. The change from frustration to curiosity was very noticeable. He withdrew a shiny silver whistle, and looked at it, puzzled.

Coach: 'How does this item relate to the situation you've been talking about?'
         There was a lengthy silence.
Coachee: 'I don't know. I don't think it has anything to do with it.'
         I allowed the coachee more thinking time.
Coach: 'What does it make you think of?'

Coachee: 'It makes me think of a football referee.'
Coach: 'And how does that relate to the challenge you're grappling with?'
Coachee: 'Well, I guess that a referee has to be decisive. Actually, even when he makes a mistake, he doesn't change his mind. He'll stick with his original decision. He can't be seen to change his mind. But it must be tough for him to see later, on TV, that he's made a howler. Having said that, though, I can understand why he doesn't change his mind. It would undermine his credibility, wouldn't it?'
Coach: 'Yes, you're right. I guess he would need to stick with his decisions.'
Coachee: 'The players give him grief, and that is even though they know that he won't change his decision. If they thought he would change his mind, that would be even worse.'
Coach: 'Is there anything about this idea that could be helpful in your situation?'
Coachee: 'Well, the idea of sticking to one's decision isn't a world away from following through on commitments, I guess. The way to overcome procrastination is to stick to my own decision to do something.'
           He looked at the whistle for a few moments.
Coachee: 'I think that the idea of sticking to a decision, no matter what happens, even if it's the wrong decision, is relevant. I need to take a page out of a referee's book.'

This exploration led to a decision to commit to only one thing at a time, and follow through on it, no matter what. The coachee decided to test his ability to stick to his commitments by setting himself one important task between coaching sessions. Gradually, he was able to change his own view that he was a 'procrastinator'. This had a positive effect on the pressure that he was putting on himself.

Friendly advice

Resources

• None

Activity

This is a simple technique that can have a significant impact. If the coachee is finding it difficult to generate options, ask her what advice she would give to somebody (eg. sister, friend, colleague) in the same situation. The question can be phrased like this: 'If a good friend of yours was in a very similar situation, and came to you for help, what advice would you give her?' This technique can overcome some of the negative self-talk that the coachee may be experiencing. By sidestepping any internal dialogue which is insisting that the coachee is 'stuck' or 'does not know the answer', she is liberated to think about the situation in another context.

When it can be helpful

This activity can change the dynamic during the Options stage. See Video 11.5.

Deserted island

Resources

• Photo of a deserted island

Activity

Show the photo of the deserted island, asking the coachee to imagine that she and the other person being discussed in the coaching conversation were to be stranded on the island. When creating the scene, add some richness to the story so that you can engage the coachee's imagination. The culmination of the story should be that the coachee and the other person end up washed ashore on a desert island. Ask the coachee to imagine how they would get on. How would they interact? How would they work together (or not) to survive on the island? The purpose of this activity is to explore any personal dynamics between the coachee and the other person, outside the professional context. The coach's role, as always, is to listen attentively to the coachee's exploration of this imaginary story. It can often bring to the fore the nature of the relationship in a way that can help the coachee to understand the source of any difficulties. In some situations, the relationship needs to be improved before the coachee can continue to pursue her goals.

When it can be helpful

This activity can be helpful during the Reality phase when the topic relates to the coachee's relationship with someone else.

Conclusion

In this chapter, we have considered a number of conversation-based activities that may help to inspire new ideas during various phases of the coaching process. It has been suggested that coaches require a certain level of confidence to introduce activities into coaching conversations. One of the best ways to become more confident about the use of activities is to try some of these with willing participants. If you know of others who are learning to coach, they would be ideal partners for this. It may be helpful to start by using the coaching activities that align with your own learning preferences. Once you are coaching, however, it is important to select the type of activity that will be of most value to the coachee. This concept will be explored further in Chapter 15. We will now turn our attention to drawing-based activities.

12
INSPIRING CREATIVITY: LET'S DRAW

This chapter will propose a number of pen-and-paper activities that can be used during coaching conversations. These drawing activities allow coachees to explore their ideas more fully and can sometimes provide a welcome break from the hard thinking and reflection necessary during coaching conversations. Pen-and-paper activities can also generate tangible items to 'take away' from coaching conversations. These can act as 'aide-memoires' or reminders of the conversation.

Storyboarding

Resources

- Sheet of white paper or flip chart paper
- Colour pens
- Post-it notes

Activity

The coach can introduce the activity by explaining how storyboarding is used to prepare for marketing campaigns or as part of film-making. A storyboard looks like a cartoon strip, with each frame containing a drawing. Storyboards are chronological, showing a series of events one frame at a time. For the purposes of this activity, six or eight frames are usually sufficient and it is preferable if the coach can provide a pre-drawn set of empty frames.

The first step is to ask the coachee to draw a representation of the current situation in the first frame. The current situation will have been discussed in the Reality stage of the GROW process. With this and all the other drawing activities it will be important to reassure the coachee about the perceived quality of the drawings. The drawings or sketches need to be meaningful to the coachee and will not be evaluated in any other context.

Once the drawing of the current situation is completed, the coach should ask the coachee to explain its significance. The coach can ask questions or share observations about how the current situation has been represented. The next stage is for the coachee to complete the final frame by drawing a visual representation of her goal (which will have been identified in the Goal stage). Allow the coachee as long as is needed to complete her drawing. Once this is completed, provide time for the coachee to explain the significance of the drawing. Ask the coachee to elaborate if necessary, as it is important that the coachee describes the desired future state as vibrantly as possible.

At this point, you will have the desired future state in the final frame and an image of the current reality in the first frame. Now the coachee is given an opportunity to quickly sketch in the missing frames, showing what types of things must happen to get from the first frame to the last frame. This is best done on post-it notes. For each blank frame, the coachee can sketch the missing step on a post-it note, before placing each post-it note in order. Using post-it notes allows the coachee to rearrange the order of the events if this is helpful. The process of sketching and drawing the intervening frames can be done during the coaching session or completed at home, in between meetings.

When it can be helpful

This activity can be helpful during the Options stage, supporting the coachee to consider the steps necessary to move closer to her goal. It is also an engaging way of thinking about what needs to happen next. The comic strip format is well-known, and therefore it can seem easier to complete the missing frames.

Thought shower

Resources

- Sheet of flipchart paper
- Flipchart pens

Activity

Many coachees may already be familiar with the notion of the thought shower (previously known as a 'brainstorm'). However, it is important to reiterate the instructions for this activity. The coachee should jot down as many ideas as possible within the given time allocation. When used during a coaching conversation, a coachee would be expected to focus on generating as many options as possible. Ideas should not be censored or evaluated at this stage. The purpose is to capture as many ideas as possible. The coach should set a challenging time constraint for the activity. This will keep the activity purposeful and energetic.

Once the time period has elapsed, the coachee should be asked to consider all the ideas that have been captured on the flipchart paper. This time, the aim is to narrow down the focus to a handful of implementable options. The coachee should either circle or cross out options after considering each one separately. Before circling or crossing off ideas, the reasons for doing this should be shared with the coach. This process is repeated until between three and six ideas remain. The coachee is then asked to decide how she would like to select between the options that are still under consideration. Using the agreed evaluation method, the coachee must now select one or two options that will be pursued.

When it can be helpful

This activity works best during the Options stage. The thought shower can include many ideas that the coachee may have not mentioned in conversation because of the pressure of jotting down as many ideas as possible within a short period of time. Talking through options without such an activity usually results in the coachee evaluating the ideas before verbalising them. As with other activities in this section, the flipchart paper will serve as a reminder of the discussion.

Missing steps

Resources

- Sheet of A3-sized paper
- Post-it notes
- Colour pencils

Activity

This is another version of the storyboarding activity. Provide the coachee with a piece of blank A3-sized paper, and ask her to draw her desired future outcome in the top right corner. Allow the coachee as much time as necessary to do this task. Once this is complete, ask the coachee to explain the drawing to you. Ask questions that require the coachee to elaborate on the desired future outcome (e.g. 'What is the significance of...').

The coachee should then draw a step in the bottom lefthand corner. In this space, ask the coachee to list all the strengths and resources available to her currently. Provide supportive comments and encourage the coachee to come up with as many as possible.

Once this is complete, the task is to connect the bottom step to the desired future outcome, using post-it notes arranged as steps. Here, the coachee may be asked to think of all the necessary steps and complete many post-it notes for arrangement later. On the other hand, some coachees may prefer to be reflective, thinking of the steps in order. Either approach works well as long as the coachee is supported to generate enough steps to get from the current reality to the goal. Once the post-it notes are in place, each can be given a target date (a date by which the step will be completed).

This activity is a very engaging, visual way of considering what is needed to get from point A (current reality) to point B (goal or desired future state). Post-it notes are always helpful because they can be discarded or rearranged as plans are made. The outcome of this activity can act as an action plan for use in future coaching sessions.

When it can be helpful

This activity is useful in the Options stage as a way of generating ideas. It can also help in the process of planning the order in which things should be done.

Drawing the metaphor

Resources

- A3-sized sheet of paper
- Colour pens

Activity

If the coachee uses an interesting or rich analogy, simile or metaphor, pause and ask her to draw it on a sheet of A3-sized paper. It is helpful to explain that exploring metaphors can be fruitful during coaching conversations. Often, drawing the metaphor can lead to additional insights. Once the drawing is complete, discuss various options and possibilities. The coach should ask questions about the drawing out of curiosity. The purpose of this activity is to allow the coachee to explore her thinking much more deeply and freely than she normally would. In my experience, talking about the metaphor is often easier than discussing the issue that it represents (see Videos 12.4 and 12.5).

When it can be helpful

Drawing the metaphor is most helpful during the Reality phase. The process of drawing it allows both coach and coachee to comment and ask questions about the metaphor, thus increasing awareness about the situation and the coachee's perception of it.

Story from Practice

In a coaching session with a teacher who had been offered a job in a different school, the coachee made a comment about feeling that she was 'out at sea'. Taking the new job would have required a relocation and the coachee was feeling uncertain about the implications her move would have on the school (her Year 6 class in particular) and her family (her children had just started secondary school). Because the coachee was finding it difficult to express her feelings, I asked her what she thought of drawing the metaphor she had just used so that we could explore it further. I volunteered that I thought it might be helpful. As we both felt a bit 'stuck' in the conversation (she wanted to accept the job but was not prepared to 'let people down'), she was glad to take a break from it. The tension eased as I produced a sheet of large paper and some colouring pens.

'What should I draw?' she asked.

'Anything you like. How about starting with being "out at sea"?' Although she claimed that she was 'not good at drawing', she was very artistic and drew a raft, bobbing on the ocean. As she drew, she explained what she was doing. 'It's a raft, not a boat. It feels flimsy, bobbing very lightly on the ocean.' She changed her mind about the ocean, and drew larger waves around the raft. 'There are waves, but the raft can manage these.' 'What about you?' I asked. She drew herself on the raft, standing in the middle. She gave herself a cartoon face with a straight line for a mouth. 'What is that face saying?' I asked. 'It's determination,' she said. She then drew some sharks (just the fins), not around the raft, but further in the distance.

Coach: 'Tell me about the sharks.'
Coachee: 'These sharks don't want me to venture out any further. I think they'll knock me off the raft.'
Coach: 'And where are you going?'

The coachee drew a tiny island in the distance with a castle on it. She drew a flag on top.

Coachee: 'I need to get there.'
Coach: 'What's it like there?'
          She smiled as she talked about what it was like on the island with the castle and I could see her eyes shine.
Coach: 'So, you're on a raft. The raft can manage the rough seas that it is in, but there are sharks just beyond, and you're worried that they may tip the raft over. But in the distance there's an island with a castle that you seem determined to get to. What are your options?'
Coachee: 'I guess I could just brave it out and go through. But I don't feel well-protected. And I know the sharks will do their best to stop me. They don't want me to reach the castle. And there's something else that I haven't drawn.'
          The coachee now drew another island. There were people on the island, waving. It was sunny, and the sea was calm.
Coach: 'Why are they waving?'
Coachee: 'Some are wishing me well, others are waving asking me to come back to the island. That's the real problem, not the sharks. I'm closer to the shore of

this island.' She pointed at the one with the people waving. 'This island is comfortable, it's warm, people want me to stay here because they like me. And I like it, too.' She become emotional, and was quiet for a few minutes. 'If I go any further on this raft, I might not be able to get back to them.' She seemed to finish her story. I thought it would be helpful to continue.

Coach: 'Sticking with the metaphor for a bit longer, what options can you think of?'

Coachee: 'Well, I can just stay here (pointing at raft) and wait for better weather,' she answered.

Coach: 'Anything else?'

Coachee: 'I could wait for the sharks to go somewhere else.'

Coach: 'Assuming that you're on the raft, what else could you do?'

Coachee: 'I could attempt the crossing, but I don't have any supplies or any protection. I guess I could try to get more supplies? Or I could wait for a passing ship to escort me. Or I could go back... But the island is too comfortable. I'm afraid that if I go back to the island, I will never have the courage to set off again, especially if I turn back now. But I guess that I have seen the island and the castle now. I know it's there, because I can see it from here (pointing at the raft). I couldn't see it from here' (pointing at the 'home' island). She became more animated at this point. 'Yes! I can go back to the island and build a better raft, with more supplies. Actually, I *should* go back and build a boat so that even if the sharks wanted to stop me, they wouldn't be able to. And most people on the island *do* actually want me to get across to the island with the castle, so they will be there to help me! Rather than risk everything now, I will get back to shore, take some time to enjoy being on the island and build the boat at the same time. And I will be more useful *on the* island rather than bobbing around on the ocean in between islands. Now I know there is this island with a castle, I won't change my mind about making the journey.' She seemed relieved, and even ended her story with a laugh: 'And I'll be packing my harpoon!'

Having drawn being 'out at sea', we then returned to the action planning stage. She would not accept the job now but wanted to commit to another year at her current school. However, she decided to undertake new tasks and school-wide challenges that would strengthen her CV. She identified an appropriate time for a relocation that would cause minimum disruption to her partner and children, and therefore knew when she should start applying for senior roles that she was interested in. According to the coachee, 'I didn't realise until I drew it, but the real issue wasn't the sharks at all!'

Back of envelope

Resources

- Regular size envelope for small letters
- Pen

Activity

In this activity, the coach presents an envelope, inviting the coachee to write on the back of it. Usually, there are automatically 'areas' on the back of an envelope (including the flap), which can help the coachee to separate ideas. Importantly, there is only limited space, so the coachee will have to be selective about her ideas and present them succinctly. At the end of the session, the envelope becomes a good artifact to take away as a record of the session. It is less likely to get lost, and the shape makes it easier to carry without folding.

When it can be helpful

This pen-and-paper activity can be particularly effective at the end of the Options phase when the coachee has *too many* ideas about what to do next. It can also be used during the Will phase when it would be beneficial for the coachee to clearly and briefly define what she is prepared to commit to.

Letter from the future

Resources

- Letter-writing paper
- Envelope
- Pen

Activity

The coachee is asked to write a letter to herself from a point in the future (e.g. ten years from now). Ask the coachee to assume that she has been successful in achieving her goal (which is the topic of the coaching conversation). In the letter, the coachee's future self should write to the coachee's present self, giving advice about how to manage the current situation. Although letter-writing may be a dying art, encourage the coachee to get into the spirit of the exercise, writing the future date at the top, starting with a salutation and concluding with a signature from the future self. Assure the coachee that this is a confidential letter, and that not even you, as the coach, will know what the letter contains. You will not ask her to read it out, although you will ask if there was any interesting advice in the letter. In your role as coach, you will need to decide what to do during the writing time. It can be helpful to leave the room for about ten minutes during this activity.

When the letter has been completed, provide an envelope for the coachee. She may wish to keep the letter as a reminder of the advice, or perhaps even lock it away and re-read it in ten years!

Wait for the coachee to put the letter away, and ask 'So, were there any useful ideas in that letter?' At the end of the coaching session, ask the coachee how helpful the letter-writing activity was.

When it can be helpful

This activity can be helpful when the coachee is facing a morally challenging decision. The letter-writing allows her to reflect on a time when the decision will have been taken, and the length of time (e.g. ten years) gives her the distance to consider the situation relatively dispassionately.

Mind map

Resources

- Paper
- Pen

Activity

The use of mind maps (Buzan, 2002) has become relatively widespread, both in business and in schools. It is often a good way to engage a coachee. Mind mapping involves drawing a spider diagram of a person's thinking. The coachee can note or draw a small representation of the goal in the centre of the paper. Then the coachee can draw a line from this to the first option that comes to mind. Once this is written down, any further thoughts that emerge as a result of this can be represented as offshoots of this option (and so on). Once this option has been explored fully, the coachee should go back to the central goal and consider a second option (and so on). What is powerful about this method is that people are usually drawn to filling the sheet of paper, and therefore tend to generate more creative ideas to fill parts of the sheet that look relatively empty. Of course, this activity can be done without a coach present, so the coach should add value by asking questions and providing positive feedback about the completion of the task. When the coachee is satisfied with the drawing, the coach should ask the coachee to summarise the key options that have been identified.

When it can be helpful

Mind mapping is especially useful in the Options phase of the coaching process. This activity is best used with coachees who are aware of the technique. This can also be a helpful activity to recommend to coachees prior to the first meeting. Coachees can be asked to draw a mind map of their topic to bring along with them as a starting point for discussion.

Hot air balloon

Resources

- A3-sized paper
- Post-it notes (various colours)
- Colour pens

Activity

This activity is helpful for generating options and evaluating them. Provide a large sheet of paper with a hot air balloon drawn on it. The drawing should be in the centre of the page, and can be drawn in a cartoon style (unless you are an artist, in which case, here's a chance to use your skill!).

Ask the coachee to imagine that she will be taking off in this balloon with all of her great ideas and options. The activity is meant to generate as many ideas and options as possible, so the coachee should jot these down on post-it notes. There will be a chance to choose which ones the coachee would like to take in the hot air balloon with her at a later stage. Initially, the coachee should be encouraged to write down all of the options that she can think of. If it is helpful, suggest that the coachee may want to colour code the options in some way, using differently coloured post-it notes.

The coach's role is to push the coachee to come up with many options, and can ask questions to help generate these:

'What else could you do?'
'What other things can you think of?'
'Are there any other options that you have already tried?'
'What might other people do in this situation?'

Once the task is complete, if there are more than ten options, ask the coachee which five she would like to place in the balloon, inviting her to consider each and then place the chosen ones in the basket. Ask the coachee to explain her reasons for selecting the five options as she places them in the basket.

Then, you should inform the coachee that there is an additional factor that you had not mentioned: she needs to be in the balloon too. Ask the coachee to draw a representation of herself on a post-it note. Once it is drawn, ask her to imagine that for the balloon to fly, there is only space for her and three of the five options. Another selection process should follow.

Finally, the coachee should develop an action plan for one of the post-it notes remaining in the basket. The other options should be kept as alternatives while the chosen option is pursued.

When it can be helpful

This can be a visually appealing activity which can support a coachee through the Options and Will stages, including the generation and evaluation of options. As with the other pen-and-paper activities shared here, the finished piece of paper can be a helpful visual reminder of the conversation and selected options.

Explanation on Twitter

Resources

- Smartphone or tablet device

Activity

The coachee should create a Twitter message (140 characters) that explains the current situation. Ask the coachee to write this out directly onto a smartphone or tablet device.

When it can be helpful

This can be very helpful during the Reality phase. It allows the coachee to distill what is really at the heart of the situation.

Conclusion

The pen-and-paper activities shared in this chapter can energise a coaching session, provide new insights and provide the coachee with strong visual images and aide-memoires of what has been discussed. It is a matter of personal preference but I would recommend that coaches explain why they are introducing pen-and-paper activities before asking coachees to engage with them. Doing so prepares the coachee for the activity, allows the coach to seek permission and builds confidence in the process.

13
INSPIRING CREATIVITY: LET'S PLAY

In the previous chapter, we considered a number of activities requiring pen and paper. Many coachees enjoy the opportunity to really get 'into' their topic by starting to draw or write it out. The most energetic coaching sessions can feel like a flurry of post-it notes and flipchart paper!

Going back to concepts discussed in the 'Beyond behaviour: exploring our thinking' (Chapter 8), sometimes changing the *doing* can lead to a change in the *thinking*. In addition, we know that we all have different learning styles, and kinaesthetic coachees may enjoy some of the activities presented in this chapter. In fact, if we know that we can learn in many different ways, it seems limiting to exclude our bodies from coaching conversations. As we will discuss later, it is not safe to assume that matching activities during coaching sessions to the learning styles of the coachees is *necessarily* a good thing. However, it is a great way to build rapport and engage the coachee, especially during the early stages of a coaching relationship.

The following activities require some physical engagement by the coachee (and sometimes the coach).

Perceptual positions

Resources

- Additional chair
- Props (as appropriate)

Activity

This activity should be explained to the coachee before inviting her to participate.

The activity 'Perceptual positions' (originally outlined by De Lozier and Grinder, 1987) is often used in coaching and can help to broaden the way in which the coachee perceives relationships. This is a slightly adapted version of the activity. Three chairs should be available in the coaching space. The coach should initiate proceedings by explaining that the purpose of the activity is to explore different ways of understanding the situation. The three perspectives to be explored are:

1. the coachee's own perspective;
2. the perspective of a significant other person;
3. the perspective of an impartial observer.

For the success of this activity, it is essential that the coachee embraces each role as fully as possible. This involves moving from chair to chair and speaking in the first person from each position.

After the coach has explained the process, the coachee should start by remaining in her chair and presenting the situation from her perspective. At this point, she should not be concerned with what others may think. It is a confidential opportunity to say what she *does* think, rather than what she believes others might want to hear. It may be helpful to give the coachee a time window for this (e.g. 'You have ten minutes for this part of the activity'). The coach should listen attentively (as always) and ensure that the coachee presents only her personal view of the situation. It is especially important for the coach to be completely non-judgemental during this segment, as the coachee should feel comfortable being entirely honest about what she is thinking and feeling. If the coachee refers to the perceptions of others, the coach should remind her that there will be an opportunity to talk about this later in the activity. Once this is completed, the coachee should be thanked for any honesty that has been exhibited and then asked to move to another chair. It should be explained that the other chair represents the 'other person' in the situation. The coachee needs to get herself into the mindframe of the other person as much as possible. For example, it might be interesting to ask the coachee to sit in the chair the way the other person would sit in it. From this chair, she should present the same situation, but from the point of view of the other person. The coach should ensure that the coachee gets into character as much as possible (e.g. the coachee should use the pronouns 'I' and 'me' to talk about the situation). Any lapses should be challenged immediately. The coachee should use personal pronouns when in the position of the 'other' (e.g. 'How *my* manager sees *me* is very important. *I* want to feel that *I'm* appreciated at work' rather than 'Liz worries about how she is perceived by her manager. She always wants to feel appreciated'). Again, a time frame is useful here. Finally, the coachee should be asked to move away from both chairs and stand at a distance from them. The coach can join the coachee, standing next to her. Looking at the chairs, the coach should ask the coachee to consider what both parties have said, getting into the mind of a completely impartial stranger. Ask the coachee to imagine that the stranger were to observe both parties having a conversation about this topic. What would the stranger see? This usually takes less time, but it can be a moment of realisation for the coachee, so no time limits should be set. When the coach and coachee retake their original seats, the activity should be reviewed, with special focus on what was learned.

When it is helpful

When the coaching topic relates to a relationship or an interaction with another person. This is especially powerful when the coachee struggles to be able to understand the other person's position. This activity is effective when there is a strong relationship between the coach and coachee.

Variations

Rather than the 'impartial stranger', it can sometimes be interesting to ask the coachee to sit in the coach's chair (you'll need to move to another chair) and think about what the coach might have noticed during this activity. The coachee can simply be asked 'what are you noticing?' This provides an opportunity for the coachee to reflect on her thoughts and also raise any moments that she found significant.

Modelling clay

Resources

- Modelling clay
- Sheet of paper

Activity

Provide the coachee with modelling clay, asking her to shape it in a way that represents the current situation. The coachee should be given a piece of modelling clay with very little instruction. The coachee does not need to make it look like anything. She can simply mould it into a shape. When the coachee has finished moulding the clay, the coach should ask her to think about how it relates to her own situation. The modelling clay can be placed on a sheet of paper and kept in view for the duration of the coaching session.

When it is helpful

This activity can work particularly well in the Reality stage and can provide insights about the current situation.

During one coaching session with an executive in the public sector, the coachee felt 'stuck'. We had been talking about the coachee's perception of current reality for about 30 minutes and he did not seem to be any clearer about what was making him feel 'stuck' in his professional role. He was unable to put his finger on what was causing tension between him and some of his colleagues at work. The general difficulty being discussed was that the 'good will' of colleagues was necessary for the coachee to complete his own projects. Unless they completed their tasks in good time, the coachee would be unable to meet his own deadlines and this was having a broader impact across his department. The coachee was getting frustrated and I felt just as 'stuck' as the coachee. I could not see how to bring more clarity to the situation. I proposed a creative activity, partly to open the opportunity for new insights but also to reduce the frustration that we were both feeling. I took out a small tub of modelling clay and handed it to him, suggesting we take a short 'break' from the conversation. I asked him to mould it into any shape that felt meaningful to him. It took him less than five minutes to create a small, well-shaped cube. He placed it on the table next to him. He looked pleased with the creation. I praised his work and asked, 'What is it?'

'I'm not sure. I guess it's a box. Or maybe it's a dice,' he said, picking it up and rolling it. The mood was certainly lighter than when we were stuck just prior to the activity.

'What is significant about it in relation to our topic today?'

Weighing it in his hand, he said, 'Well, maybe I feel like I'm trapped ... in a box? Maybe it feels like I'm stuck inside there and I can't get out?' He looked at me to see if he was on the right track. I didn't know, so I just waited for him to continue. 'Yes. I guess it could mean that I feel trapped in a box ...'

'Anything else?' I wondered aloud.

'Actually, boxes and squares are boring, right? Maybe I am a bit "square" at work. I know that I like to stick to protocols and procedures. And I sometimes wonder whether others might find me a bit "boxy". The other thing is that I'm a bit more like a box than a bouncy ball. Most of my colleagues would have probably created a bouncy ball with that piece of modelling clay. They're mostly "happy go lucky" people, bouncing from one thing to another. Maybe I'm a box in a room full of bouncy balls ...' At this point, he softened the corners of the cube. 'Maybe I can soften the corners, without becoming a ball – just a box with smoother corners!'

This is only part of a longer conversation. The use of modelling clay helped to provide the coachee with a new perspective. The 'stuckness' related to the difference in outlooks between him and his colleagues. Amongst other options, he thought of involving these colleagues in projects from the outset, engaging in more work-related social events and 'popping in' to see colleagues to talk about 'live' projects.

At the end of the session, the coachee asked whether he could take the cube (with softened edges) away with him. He wanted to keep it on his desk to remind him of the conversation. He reported that his 'A-ha!' moment ('A-ha!' moments will be discussed in Chapter 15) was the realisation that he could 'soften his edges' without changing into a ball (which would have felt inauthentic).

Story from Practice

Building blocks

Resources

- Building blocks (e.g. Lego)
- Some figurines, characters or plastic toy animals

Activity

Ask the coachee to spend ten minutes with the building blocks to represent the current situation she is facing. It can be helpful to include characters or toy animals that can be used to represent people involved in the situation. Allow the coachee to work on this herself for at least ten minutes before commenting or getting involved. Unless the coachee requests more time, wrap up the activity on time and then ask her how helpful the activity was. If she has found it unhelpful, the coach can just ask whether the task provided any insights. If the answer is still 'no', it is probably not worth pursuing it any further.

However, if the coachee does comment positively about the activity, first ask what the coachee learned about herself while playing with the Lego. (It's OK to use the word 'playing'!) Ask the coachee to use that learning to think about what options arise from looking at the Lego creation. If the activity resonates with the coachee, it is possible that she will use her creation as she talks about her options, moving characters, animals and building blocks around to explore different possibilities.

In this activity, ensure that the coachee is the only person handling the building blocks. It is one way of allowing the coachee to take full ownership of her situation and any options that might be generated.

When is it helpful?

This activity is helpful during the Options stage, especially if the coachee feels that she has very few choices.

Director's chair

Resources

'Director's chair' (any chair which is different from the ones used by the coach and coachee).

Activity

Tell the coachee that she will be directing a play about her own life. The play is set in the present time. Firstly, ask the coachee how she would select the person to play the main character (herself). How would the coachee (director) find the right actor to play the lead character? What will the coachee (director) be looking for?

Explain that the plot will be the summary of the Reality phase. Ask the director to briefly outline the plot, as if talking to the actors of the play. She can stand up and show them how she would like them to perform their roles. The coach should ask questions to gain a better understanding of the various roles. Finally, the director is asked to give the lead character advice about how she can deal with the situation facing her.

When is it helpful?

This activity is helpful during the Options stage, especially if the topic concerns relationships between people.

Role-play

Resources

- Props (if needed)

Activity

Many coachees (and coaches) may find the idea of role-play daunting initially. So, it is worth presenting this idea when you feel that you have established a reasonably strong relationship with the coachee. The first step is for the coach to offer to take the role of the other party. This is especially useful if the coachee would like to consider different ways of approaching an issue or topic with the other person. Again, it is important for both coach and coachee to get into their characters, using personal pronouns and trying to represent them as realistically as possible. This stage of the process is useful because it builds the confidence of the coachee (she is playing herself, and knows what this feels like). Even more importantly, it will give the coachee an opportunity to correct your portrayal of the other party (e.g. 'My line manager is always positive and optimistic. He wouldn't have highlighted the risks in that way'). By having this role-play and the following discussion, the coachee is likely to get a better sense of the nature of their relationship.

The crucial second step of this activity involves a role reversal. This can be managed very smoothly if the coachee points out that you, as the coach, are not representing the other person accurately. In this case, you can suggest that she takes on the role of the other party, with you (as the coach) taking on the role of the coachee (while she plays the other party). By requiring the coachee to put herself in the place of the other person, the activity can lead to insights about the other person's motives, thoughts and point of view.

When it can be helpful

Role-play is helpful when the topic of the coaching conversation revolves around a professional relationship at work that is getting in the way of the coachee's goals and aspirations. In the Reality phase, role-play can aid a deeper understanding of challenging relationships. In the Options phase, different ways of approaching a situation can be tested. In the Will phase, role-play can be used very effectively to 'rehearse' what the coachee has decided to do in order to prepare her for forthcoming conversations.

Story from Practice In a conversation with a middle leader in a small start-up organisation, the coachee finally decided to confront her manager about the lack of clarity about whether or not she was required to work on weekends. This had been frustrating the coachee for a few months. She worked, albeit reluctantly, on some weekends when she was given substantial pieces of work with short deadlines. At the Will stage, the coachee concluded very convincingly that her only option was to be 'open and honest' about this with her direct line manager. As we had not had much time to talk through the implications of this, I suggested that we could act it out. The coachee was enthusiastic about the activity, so I explained that we could rehearse the interaction with myself taking on the role of her manager. As agreed, she left the room. She knocked on the door, and popped her head round the door. 'Hello, Layla,' she said. I responded kindly, asking her to come in. At this point, the coachee said 'This is the difficult bit! How can I suddenly start talking about my issue with Saturdays? It won't feel right.' Although the activity was brief, it helped the coachee realise that she was not ready to do what she had thought would be her next step. As a result of this, she selected a different next step which felt more appropriate to her.

Walk and talk

Resources

None

Activity

When the topic of conversation relates to someone feeling 'stuck' or 'trapped', we have to question the logic of locking them into a room for two hours to talk about it! Of course, there are many times (probably in the majority of cases) when sitting in a room for an hour or two can provide a moment of insight. In other cases, it may be worth considering taking the coaching outdoors.

It is possible, and sometimes powerful, to have a coaching conversation when walking. There is an interesting human dynamic when two people walk next to one another that requires some type of connection. As with every coaching conversation, it will be necessary to contract before the coaching starts. There will be more distractions, and, as a coach, it may be helpful to acknowledge this. There are also some risks to confidentiality that should be considered.

For the walk and talk approach to be effective, a relatively quiet or relaxing environment is beneficial. Perhaps an art gallery, a museum, a park or even a large garden would provide an appropriate environment. Apart from the fact that the coaching takes place outdoors, the rest of the process can be exactly the same, perhaps finishing off at a cafe or a park bench to agree the way forward.

When it can be helpful

This approach can be helpful if the topic is relatively demotivating or when the coachee is frustrated because she feels 'stuck'. It can also be used for a particular stage of the coaching process. For example, 'walking and talking' may be a good way to establish the current state of play (Reality phase) or think of new ways of approaching a topic (Options phase).

Conclusion

Creativity requires new thinking. It invites people to 'do things differently', so using innovative approaches is an essential part of the coaching process. Otherwise, coaching itself can run the risk of falling into a rut. For a coachee, knowing that she will be speaking to her coach for two hours, in the same room, every month for six months can become too comfortable. As you will hopefully be thinking by now, perhaps this applies to the coach as well. A coach must be fresh, curious and interested. It is normal to be anxious in the beginning, in the same way a person might feel anxious when learning how to ride a motorcycle. It will feel a bit 'clunky'. There will be nerves. But after a while, if you like riding, you will start to look forward to getting on the motorcycle. You'll enjoy the ride. And, if after you've learned to ride, you find that you do not enjoy motorcycling, then you would probably look for something else to do. Coaching is the same.

SNAPSHOT Tips for using activities effectively during coaching conversations

1. Build your own confidence and belief in the use of activities by trying these out in practice situations.
2. Remember that the post-activity discussion is an important part of the process. In other words, exploring what the coachee learned through the activity is as valuable as the activity itself.
3. Choose the activities intentionally based on what is most helpful for the coachee. The choice of activity should be led by the desired outcome.
4. Seek permission to introduce an activity and explain why you are suggesting it.
5. Match the activity with the coachee's learning style if you are building rapport and strengthening your relationship.
6. Mismatch the activity with the coachee's learning style to challenge her and gain new insights.

PART FIVE
WAY OF BEING

 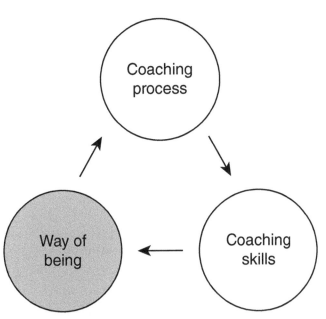
Figure 14.1 Elements of effective coaching

By this point in the book, I hope you are feeling more confident about your coaching-related skills. As you practise coaching, this sense of confidence should increase. In addition, you have learned the GROW model, one of the best-known coaching processes. Like learning to drive a car or ride a motorcycle, it may feel a bit uncomfortable at first, but you will soon be able to glide through the GROW model without having to concentrate on the process, and many of the questions you ask will emerge naturally from the coaching conversation. Practising the coaching skills will make you more fluent at asking the right kinds of questions. You will be better able to summarise in a helpful way, listen actively and share feedback with your coachees. If you think back to Chapter 2 ('Becoming a coach'), you will remember that it was proposed that there were three elements to successful coaching. The skills and the process are two of the elements. The third element relates to what has been described as a 'way of being'. Many would say that this underpinning philosophy is impossible to 'teach' on a course or in a book. While this may be true, I believe it can be learned through coaching and reflective practice. Developing the 'way of being' is probably a lifelong endeavour. In this chapter, I will describe a 'way of being' which is appropriate for coaches before proposing some attributes that you may wish to work towards.

Way of being

The phrase 'way of being' in relation to one-to-one relationships was coined by the influential humanistic psychologist, Dr Carl Rogers (1980). He founded the 'person-centred approach' and his principles continue to influence our coaching practice today.

Rogers based his thinking on two foundational premises. Firstly, he proposed that people are their own best experts. In other words, people know themselves better than others can. Secondly, he believed that people are self-actualising. This means that people naturally grow towards achieving their full potential, rather like plants which grow towards the light. These two premises led him to suggest that the role of a counsellor is to simply create the conditions in which a person can be allowed to self-actualise.

Rogers famously outlined the 'necessary and sufficient conditions' for a successful counselling relationship:

- Two persons are in psychological contact.
- The client is in a state of incongruence.
- The counsellor is congruent in the relationship.
- The counsellor experiences unconditional positive regard for the client.
- The counsellor experiences an empathic understanding of the client's internal frame of reference and endeavours to communicate this experience to the client.
- This communication is achieved to a minimal degree.
  (Adapted from Rogers, 1957: 95)

Bearing in mind that Rogers developed this set of necessary and sufficient conditions for counselling relationships (he used the word 'therapist' instead of 'counsellor' in the bulletpoints above) rather than coaching relationships, which are still relevant and appropriate for us as coaches?

1. There must be a good relationship between the coach and the coachee.
2. The coachee must want to make a change.
3. The coach must be authentic in her interactions with the coachee.
4. The coach's positive regard for the coachee must be unconditional.
5. The coach must demonstrate empathy.

Point 4 may need some clarification. The phrase 'the coach's positive regard for the coachee must be unconditional' means that the coach should respect the coachee and view her positively (as a human being) regardless of what she might say or do during the coaching conversation. The opposite of this would be *conditional* positive regard, meaning that a coachee would be given respect and viewed positively (as a human being) as long as she spoke and behaved in a way which met with the approval of the coach.

Based on Rogers's necessary and sufficient conditions for therapeutic change, it is proposed that the five revised 'conditions' listed above may be necessary for successful coaching to take place. There is currently debate about whether Rogers's conditions, by themselves, are *sufficient* for change to occur. In my view, when translated into a coaching context, the conditions are *necessary* but may not be sufficient. To put it another way, the conditions are necessary, but other things need to happen as well. I have argued in this book that three elements are needed:

- A clear process managed by the coach.
- A set of coaching-related skills.
- A 'way of being' for coaching (including the five revised conditions listed above).

Partnership principles

Rogers spent a lifetime explaining and elaborating the notion and it is difficult to convey the exact sense of what is meant by 'way of being' in summary.

FIND OUT MORE

The concept of 'way of being' is described in detail in Carl Rogers's book, *A Way of Being* (1980). If you would like to explore this notion further, I recommend reading this book when you have some quality time for learning and reflection.

A leading educationalist, Dr Jim Knight, has very helpfully provided a more concrete description of the 'way of being' necessary for coaching conversations. According to Knight, every coaching interaction should be underpinned by a certain set of 'partnership principles' (2011). According to Knight, good coaching should be an authentic partnership between two people of equal status. The principles are equality, choice, dialogue, praxis, voice, reciprocity and reflection. Each is listed below, with a brief description of the principle and a consideration of how this might inform our coaching practice.

Equality

For us as coaches, the word 'partnership' denotes a relationship between equals. Each partner's thoughts, beliefs and feelings are held to be valuable while recognising that each person is different. At the heart of this notion of equality is a clear commitment to respect one another. In an equal relationship based on mutual respect, one partner will not impose her will on another.

Implication for practice

Ensure that you create a sense of partnership and equality in all interactions with the coachee. As a coach, you must see the coachee as being of equal value (and demonstrate this to her). When decisions need to be made, they should be discussed between both parties. Any suggestions from the coach should be followed by checking what the coachee thinks of the idea. If you are meeting regularly, ensure that you are doing so in a neutral space, or that you alternate between meeting in a place that is convenient for the coachee and then a place that is convenient for the coach. Seemingly trivial details like the arrangement or selection of chairs should demonstrate the principle of equality. Both chairs should be identical or similar. The moment that one party sits on a leather chair and the other is perched on a stool, the principle of equality has been contravened. This concept of equality also applies to the responsibility of both parties. There is a shared responsibility for a successful coaching session. The coach is responsible for the process, and the coachee is responsible for the topic of the conversation.

Choice

Choice is a critical factor in the type of relationship we are talking about here. Both parties should feel that they have genuine choices. In coaching, one person cannot make decisions for the other. The coach must respect the autonomy of the coachee, and this means that the coachee must make her own choices.

Implication for practice

When coaching, the fact that the coachee should make her own choices should be made explicit. For example, coming to coaching should be a choice. This should not be imposed. It should also be made clear to the coachee that she has a choice about who her coach is. When agreeing the coaching contract, both parties should be clear that they are able to withdraw from the coaching relationship if it is not working. To make this a *real* choice, it should be possible to withdraw without having to give any reason. This principle also means that the coachee can choose any action that she thinks is appropriate at the end of the session. This includes the freedom to make 'bad' choices. Many coaches are concerned about allowing the coachee to make the 'wrong' choice. There is no such thing. By the end of the conversation, the coachee will have considered a broad range of options and will have had time to think through the consequences. Therefore, her choice of next step should be respected. For the coachee, having choices makes her feel more autonomous.

Dialogue

Although I have suggested earlier that a coach should only be speaking for about 20% of the time, the nature of a coaching conversation is a dialogue. This means that both parties are engaged in the conversation, and both recognise that they are learning together as they explore ideas. According to Knight, 'Dialogue is talking with the goal of digging deeper and exploring ideas together' (2011: 38).

Implications for practice

As coaching is a dialogue between equals, it is important that issues are considered together. It is entirely appropriate (and more helpful in some cases) if both parties are exploring a situation about which neither person has expert knowledge. This creates a genuine dialogue between two people. Everything that the coachee says should be considered carefully, and the coach must not reject, ignore or belittle any statement. At the heart of the concept of dialogue is listening respectfully to what the other person says. Dialogue requires both parties to fully 'hear' what the other person has said before intervening or presenting their own views. For the coach, this means limiting interruptions. This also means that the coach should not be planning the next question or activity while the coachee is speaking. Such an approach may lead to short silences when the coachee has finished sharing her thoughts. And that is OK. It demonstrates that you were listening to her and thinking about what was said.

Praxis

Coaching is powerful because of its focus on the application of learning in the *real world*. In other words, coaching is not a theoretical exercise even though much of it can be spent talking about ideas. According to Knight, coachees should have 'opportunities to think about how to apply new ideas to their real-life practices' (2011: 43).

Implications for practice

Praxis is the application of learning into practice. It is a shared responsibility of both coach and coachee to ensure that the coaching conversation eventually results in a change in the coachee's behaviour or performance. For the coach, this means ensuring that practical next steps are considered in the final part of a coaching session. The start of subsequent coaching sessions can be initiated by reviewing what the coachee has *done* differently since the previous meeting. The focus on the implications of the coaching discussion on the lived experience of the coachee makes the conversation more meaningful. Questions such as 'How will this play out in your workplace?', 'What are the consequences for the way in which you interact with your colleagues?' or 'If you were to proceed with this option, how would this impact on your project?' will help to highlight the relationship between the coaching discussion and the 'real' world.

Voice

This principle reminds us that both parties in the relationship should be able to express their points of view honestly. It is important that the coachee feels comfortable expressing her thoughts and aspirations. 'If partners are equal, if they choose what they do and do not do, they should be free to say what they think, and their opinions should count' (Knight, 2011: 34).

Implications for practice

Coaches have a prime responsibility to encourage the coachee to voice her thoughts and emotions. In some situations, a coachee will be voicing her concerns or aspirations for the first time, and this voice needs to be encouraged. This is why coaches must remain non-judgemental, being open to whatever the coachee may say. Any judgement or criticism from the coach may lead to the coachee 'losing' her voice. She may start to censor her thoughts if she fears a judgemental response. For coaching to be successful, coachees should be able to provide honest feedback about the coach and the coaching relationship. A coach's genuine openness to feedback encourages the coachee to share her thoughts and feelings more openly.

Reciprocity

The principle of reciprocity posits that both parties should benefit from a coaching conversation. This means that both coach and coachee can enter into a coaching conversation expecting to learn from each other and develop as a result. Knight puts it this way: 'Reciprocity is the belief that each learning interaction is an opportunity for everyone to learn – an embodiment of the saying, "when one teaches, two learn"' (2011: 44).

Implications for practice

In practice, both coach and coachee should emerge from a coaching session feeling better, in some way, from the interaction. This approach enhances the sense of equality. As the title of this chapter suggests, the 'way of being' is essentially about bringing our 'humanness' to the fore. As human beings, we learn through interaction. We are social animals. So, as a coach, it is important to see each coaching conversation as an opportunity to learn. The primary purpose of the coachee is to learn more about herself, the situation that she is in and what she might achieve. But it is also a learning experience for the coach who can learn about herself, the way in which humans engage with challenges and opportunities and about the coaching process. A good practical way of capturing this is to note down at least one thing that you learned as a result of each coaching conversation.

Reflection

The appropriate 'way of being' for coaches should encourage reflection, both for the coach and the coachee. Through her behaviour and by applying the principles, a coach can create a valuable thinking space for her coachees.

Implications on practice

As you will soon discover, we, as coaches, do genuinely learn during our coaching. We learn about ourselves. We learn about others. And we discover a great deal about what it means to be human. I would recommend capturing your learning in a coaching journal.

Coaching journal   Activity

One of the most helpful ways to develop your own 'way of being', is to capture your thoughts in a coaching journal. The purpose of this journal is to keep a record of your own thoughts, feelings and experiences as you start to coach. For one thing, this will reinforce the principle of reciprocity, because you will be acknowledging that you are learning from each coaching session. The best form of professional development for coaches is reflective practice. This will be discussed further in Chapter 16, 'Reflecting on practice'. See below for a proposed format for coaching logs.

1. Make a note of your thoughts and feelings prior to a coaching session, and just after a coaching session. These thoughts can take the form of an essay or simply a list of bullet points.
2. The layout can include a few sentences about the overall purpose of the coaching session. This should be followed by your own reflections about the session. Each entry should conclude with a few statements about what you have learned and what you will do differently as a result. You might want to lay out the coaching logs in the following format.

- Date:
- Purpose of coaching session:
- Personal reflections:
- My learning:
- What I will do differently:

Confidentiality: Remember to completely anonymise the entries. Mark the date of your journal entry, but not the date of the coaching session. Also ensure that you do not use any names or provide any information which could identify the coachee. It is possible that notebooks can be lost and computer programs can be hacked. In order to ensure the confidentiality of your coaching conversations, write in your journal in such a way as not to jeopardise this confidentiality, even if the coaching logs were to be compromised.

Story from Practice

The partnership principles

When learning to become a coach, one of my fears was to be confronted by a coachee who was not willing to be coached. I now find such situations a much richer learning experience for both the coach and the coachee. When reflecting on a challenging coaching conversation, I was able to see how the partnership principles helped to create the right conditions for a successful outcome. The story below is taken from my own learning journal with details changed in order to protect anonymity. The notes in square brackets are my original notes as I reflected on the session.

Journal entry

I had travelled for an hour to get to the coachee's place of work. There was parking nearby, but this was underground and seemed to be designed for very small cars! It was difficult to get from the car park to the city centre office complex and I had to ask for directions. [As a coach, I arrived for the coaching session a bit frazzled. In future, I will allow an extra 15 minutes. A quick coffee somewhere would have settled my own nerves.]

I arrived at the office a few minutes early, but the secretary kept me waiting for another 10 minutes. When I met the coachee I wasn't sure whether I should apologise for lateness. I did anyway, but noted that I *had* arrived on time. [This may have come across as defensive, and was not a good way to start our interaction.]

We both looked very formal and we walked to a small room with comfortable seating and some chairs. The coachee was civil but not friendly. The coachee sat down on one of the sofas, and gestured for me to sit on a chair. He did not offer any drinks. [Another reason it would have been helpful to arrive 15 minutes early for a coffee!] I said I would prefer to sit on the sofa opposite to where he was sitting. There was a low table between us, but this did not seem like a barrier.

Before I had a chance to talk about contracting, the coachee announced: 'Before we start, there's something that I would like to tell you. I don't believe in this coaching bullshit. I am here because my line manager has instructed me to be here. I think it's a waste of my time, and you have one hour, not longer.' [Initially, I felt myself becoming defensive. Some anxiety set in. Even an hour seemed like a very long time!] So, before contracting, we had a brief chat about the situation. I reflected back that he seemed angry about being in the coaching session, and I said that it seemed like we both felt obliged to be in the room – he had been told to attend a coaching session, and I had been paid to deliver it. I asked whether he and I could agree something that would make best use of the time that we both felt we *had* to spend together. We agreed to talk for an hour, rather than the 90–120 minute session that I had been contracted to deliver. I said that we could decide whether or not to continue the coaching sessions at the end of our time together. When he said that his manager would not be happy if he rejected any further sessions, I said that I would be willing to write to the manager myself, saying that *I* did not see the value in any further sessions.

I could see a change in attitude in the coachee. We re-presented the coaching session as a pre-coaching chat which was simply a two-way conversation about whether there would be any benefit from carrying on with the coaching assignment. [If I am honest, there was also a change in me. There was less pressure on both of us, and the worst-case scenario seemed to be that the coachee would want to drop out. At this stage, I would have been quite comfortable with that outcome.] Despite this, I did go through the contracting, especially highlighting confidentiality and the fact that I would not divulge any of the conversation to the line manager. At the end of the entire process (if we did decide to continue), I said that I would have to provide a summary of the topics discussed and my simple assessment of whether the sessions were successful or not. I promised to show this to the coachee and get his approval before sending it to his line manager.

To start the coaching session, I said that he could talk about anything he liked, and that we did not need to talk about the issue for which he had been 'sent' to be coached. Again, there was a positive response. 'What shall we talk about then?' he asked. 'Anything you like,' I replied. I asked him whether he would like to tell me a bit about why he was so set against the idea of coaching.

We could have spent the full two hours talking, but we stopped after an hour, as this was part of our amended agreement. Just before the end of our 60 minutes, I reminded the coachee of our initial conversation. I said that we had agreed that we would make a decision about future sessions. I reiterated that I would be pleased to pursue any of the routes available. We could both report back to the line manager saying that we found no value in the coaching conversations, he could talk to the line manager himself and withdraw from the process, or we could agree to meet again. The only stipulation was that the next conversation would be more of a coaching conversation, and that we would need to work on the coachee's goals (as this one had been almost entirely about how the coachee felt about coaching and what had led to the current situation). Although it was grudging, the coachee said that he now thought there might be some value in coaching, checking that he would be able to set the agenda for the next coaching session.

Reflecting on session

In the face of obvious resistance to coaching, I felt that trying to pursue a traditional coaching conversation would be futile. Rather than focus on the topic (which was implied by the line manager), I chose to focus on seeing if we could build a relationship.

I was genuine in the coaching session by saying that both of us felt compelled to be there, and that neither of us was looking forward to the session. It was a bit of a risk to say that I did not want to be there either, but in the moment it was true. I had arrived a bit frazzled, I did not have a cup of coffee and I was faced by a seemingly aggressive coachee who seemed determined that the coaching session would fail. However, I did not judge the coachee, and importantly, I resisted an early instinct to put up my own defenses and barriers.

That honesty, though, changed the dynamic. It seemed like the barriers came down, and both of us were talking to each other like human beings. I was surprised at

(Continued)

(Continued)

how quickly we built a relationship, and I was able to empathise genuinely with the coachee who explained why he was angry.

At the end of the conversation, I thought that we had built a relationship but I was not sure whether further coaching sessions would be of value, and was prepared to support either decision from the coachee. At the same time, while I thought we spent our first hour together effectively building a relationship, I was clear that if we chose to pursue the coaching, future sessions would have to focus on the coachee's performance in the workplace (which is what I had been contracted to deliver). So when the coachee said, 'Yeah, I guess we could continue with the sessions,' I asked whether he thought that further sessions would be helpful to him in relation to his performance at work. He replied that he was prepared to give it a go.

As it happens, this series of coaching conversations was very successful despite the rocky start – both for the coachee and for myself as the coach. I learned so much about how people respond to negative pressure and the importance of the relationship in coaching. Even more remarkably, that coaching conversation and the way in which the coachee made decisions about his own future, influenced decisions that I took about my own professional future.

Towards a 'way of being'

I am hoping that this book has encouraged you to be self-reflective and more self-aware. This chapter has considered some 'necessary conditions' for effective coaching and we have also grappled with the concept of 'way of being' by looking at Jim Knight's partnership principles (2011).

Below, I will outline some ideal attributes for coaches based on a loose understanding of Rogers's 'way of being' (1980). Each represents a lifelong journey of development. These attributes can be considered aspirational goals for coaches. Self-awareness is important as you consider each point. You may already possess some of these attributes, others may require a lifetime of learning and development. We must be honest and humble when deciding on whether or not we need to invest time in any of the points below.

The most effective coaches are humble

Humility is an important attribute for a coach. Without humility, it is difficult to enter into equal relationships. Humility allows a person to constantly be a learner. Status games have no place in the coaching arena.

The most effective coaches are confident in their ability as coaches

While humility is an important attribute, coaches need to be confident in their coaching abilities. Confidence in our coaching ability can be picked up by the coachee. Any self-doubt on our part can be contagious.

The most effective coaches care about people

Coaches should be driven by a desire to make things better for people. Of course, many coaches earn a livelihood from this business. However, 'making things better for people' should be the primary drive, not financial gain. Coaching is a very *human* way of interacting.

The most effective coaches believe that their coachees will achieve more of their potential

The belief of the coach is an integral part of the self-belief of the coachee. Research has shown that a person's positive expectation about another person's abilities can become a self-fulfilling prophecy (Rosenthal and Jacobson, 1966, 1968).

The most effective coaches treat others with respect

Feeling respected is one of the non-negotiables of trusting relationships. In order to build long-term, successful professional relationships, coaches must respect their clients and be able to demonstrate this respect quickly and consistently. Human beings are quick to sense the absence of respect.

The most effective coaches have integrity

Coachees must trust their coaches for them to be open and honest about their feelings, thoughts, aspirations and fears. Trust is built as coachees start to recognise that their coaches always operate with integrity. And this is not just about what happens in the coaching room.

In this chapter, we have carefully considered some of the key principles and attributes of effective coaches. As I hope you will have noticed, they are based on the humanistic principles of Carl Rogers. Essentially, coaching is a humanising activity, for both coach and coachee. To become a coach is to embrace the most positive aspects of being human.

15

INSPIRING OTHERS

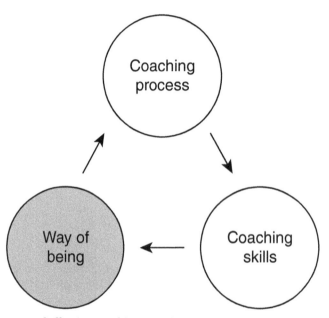

Figure 15.1 Elements of effective coaching practice

Many coachees report that they have been 'inspired' to overcome challenges, pursue their dreams and achieve their ambitions through coaching. Sometimes this inspiration is a result of the coaching relationship and a series of coaching conversations. In other situations, the inspiration emerges out of an 'A-ha!' moment which can take place within or in between coaching sessions. In this penultimate chapter, we will explore the 'A-ha!' moment specifically.

'A-ha!' moments

The 'A-ha!' moment refers to a sudden realisation or recognition that can have a lasting effect. It is the moment when a person 'gets it'. For some, it is a life-changing experience. If you have had an 'A-ha!' moment in the past, you will know how powerful it can be. Coaches and educators can be motivated by trying to create 'A-ha!' moments in their coachees and students.

In my own experience as a coach and supervisor of coaches, I have come to believe that there are a few common themes that seem to recur in discussions about 'A-ha!' moments. These are:

1. A sense of connection
2. Sharper clarity
3. A positive sensation
4. A feeling of excitement
5. Increased confidence.

'A-ha!' moments usually involve the linking of a number of disparate thoughts. Coachees have reported that it can feel like a 'fog lifting', 'a light bulb coming on', 'the moment the clouds part and the sun shines through' or a 'fireworks display lighting up the darkness'. These descriptions align well with some research into the phenomenon by Dr Erik de Haan and his colleagues (2010). Participants in the research described some critical moments in coaching with phrases such as 'lightbulb', 'a tipping point' or 'moment of realisation'. The research demonstrated that critical moments (such as the 'A-ha!' moment) can lead to coachees making significant changes (de Haan, Bertie, Day and Sills, 2010).

How to increase the likelihood of 'A-ha!' moments in coaching sessions

There are two interesting paradoxes concerning 'A-ha!' moments in coaching. Firstly, although many coaches would recognise the critical importance of these moments, very little is said about them, and even less has been written about 'A-ha!' moments in coaching. So, in this chapter, let us address this topic so that we can consider how we might be able to make 'A-ha!' moments more likely during our coaching sessions. Here, we should pause to reflect on the second paradox: the more you chase an 'A-ha!' moment, the more elusive it becomes. So rather than pushing for an 'A-ha!' moment, coaches would be well advised to focus on creating the right context for it to take place.

What About You?

Think back to an 'A-ha!' moment that you have had. How did it come about? What was the context? What factors played a part in your 'A-ha!' moment?

Creating the right context

While remaining mindful that pushing too hard for an 'A-ha!' moment may be counterproductive, it may be possible for coaches to create the context in which such moments might emerge.

Firstly, the coach should ensure that the 'necessary conditions for coaching' exist. These are listed in Chapter 14, 'Being human'. This applies to every coaching session, but it is worth reiterating here. Secondly, the coach should invest in developing a strong, trusting relationship. Research has shown that a strong relationship is the key determinant of coaching success (de Haan, 2008b). In the early stages of a coaching relationship, it is important to prioritise the relationship above anything else. Without that strong foundation, the coaching is less likely to succeed, and the chances of an 'A-ha!' moment are diminished. Thirdly, although this may be unwelcome news, discomfort is often a feature of effective coaching conversations. De Haan's research has found that there is usually some discomfort before a critical moment in coaching conversations (2008b). This means that if we have a tendency to avoid uncomfortable situations in coaching, we are minimising the chances of 'A-ha!' moments occurring.

Story from Practice

I was coaching a middle manager in a large educational organisation. She was frustrated because her staff were not supporting her during a challenging period of change. This was despite all the efforts she made to represent their views and champion the cause of her team. She explained the situation. 'I feel like I'm "piggy in the middle". Management have been clear with me about what changes they would like to see. They're irritated at the slow progress that my team and I have made. But this is because I have been consulting with people in my team throughout the process. I take the messages from our management group to my own team, and present the new initiative in as positive a way as possible. When my team (sometimes rightly) are dissatisfied with some element of the proposals, I represent this strongly to the management group. I don't know what more I can do. When I go to the management group, they see me as a troublemaker and a laggard. When I speak with my team, they are resistant and unfriendly. They cannot see that I am working for their benefit.' After exploring the discrepancy between her view of what she was doing and the response she was getting from her team, the coachee realised something. She stopped talking, and looked down. I could see tears welling up in her eyes. 'They don't trust me', she said. It was uncomfortable, and I was tempted to relieve this discomfort by suggesting that there might be other reasons for their behaviour. But instead I waited. She wiped away tears and looked up again. 'It makes sense now. I can understand why they are behaving this way. They think that I am trying to manipulate the situation – that I have already agreed to the proposals and I am just bringing them to my way of thinking. All they see is that I am away talking to senior managers at least once a week. They don't know what happens there.' Having realised why her team were behaving that way helped the coachee to plan a new strategy. The coachee was determined and upbeat. What had been a mystery now seemed clear. It allowed her to turn her attention to finding a way to rebuild the relationship with her team.

'A-ha!' moments occur when a person thinks new thoughts or connects previously disparate ideas. For this to happen, the coaching conversation is likely to enter uncharted territory, or the unknown. There will be times when both the coach and the coachee will not know what to do or think. As a coach, you must resist the temptation to return to charted territory by taking control of the situation or by telling the coachee what to do. Uncertainty during coaching conversations is a sure indication that you are entering fertile new ground – a place in which 'A-ha!' moments are more likely. It is also liberating for the coach to start to feel that 'not knowing' is acceptable. By feeling this way, we demonstrate to the coachee that it is OK for her not to know either.

In a research paper, de Haan notes that critical moments sometimes follow silences (2008a). Silences often precede new thoughts, because a silence can be an indication that the coachee is thinking. As we have seen previously, the use of silences is appropriate in coaching. It allows for quality thinking and it puts the responsibility for new ideas where it should be: with the coachee.

Finally, there are times when focusing too hard on a difficulty or barrier can heighten the feeling of being 'stuck'. Sometimes it is helpful to 'zoom out' or talk about something on the periphery of the coachee's topic. This can reduce frustration and allow for creative thoughts to emerge. Our minds can continue to think through an issue even when we are not focused on it. This explains why we sometimes wake up with the solution to something that may have been troubling us when we went to bed.

So, to create the right context for 'A-ha!' moments to occur, we should:

- ensure the existence of the necessary conditions for coaching;
- invest in the relationship between coach and coachee;
- accept that discomfort is a necessary part of the coaching process;
- be comfortable with the unknown during coaching conversations;
- use silences to encourage new thinking;
- reduce feelings of being stuck by refocusing on peripheral topics.

In addition to creating the right context, we must also encourage creativity during the coaching conversation. Firstly, a coach can encourage creativity by using the pen-and-paper, active learning and conversational activities described in Chapters 11–13 in this book. Although this may sound counterintuitive, it is sometimes better to invite a coachee to undertake activities which do not match her learning style. There may be a little bit of 'nudging' out of comfort zones required. Remember, it is likely that the coachee will already have tried her preferred problem-solving techniques before coming to coaching. When discussing possible options, the coach should not accept the first one or two options that a coachee presents. More often than not, these will be options that have been considered and tried before. Although it may feel annoying to the coachee, it is a good idea to push the coachee by continuing to ask 'What else could you do?' Often, if the coachee can answer this question straight away, she is not presenting a new idea. Finally, you need to keep faith and believe that the coachee will come up with the best solution or way forward in relation to the topic. We must not 'give up' on our coachees. The moment we provide a coachee with a solution or a way forward, there is an implied suggestion that we do not think she would be able to come up with a solution for herself.

So, to encourage creativity during a coaching conversation, we should:

- use a variety of pen-and-paper, active learning and conversational activities;
- invite the coachee to engage with an activity that does not match her preferred learning style;
- encourage the coachee to generate more than one or two options;
- believe in the ability of the coachee to identify her own way forward.

If you take into account the ideas above, creating the right context for the coachee and encouraging her to be creative, she is much more likely to experience an 'A-ha!' moment which can have a significant and lasting impact on her life.

Using a 'coaching approach'

As you practise coaching, you will improve your skills, broaden your range of questions and develop the 'way of being' discussed in this book. If you do this, I am confident that you will make a difference to the people you coach. However, people interested in this topic often talk about the idea of a 'coaching approach' which can take place beyond coaching conversations. Leaders in organisations are sometimes described as having a coaching approach when managing their teams, leading change and developing corporate cultures. Some educators report that they use a coaching approach with their classes or groups of students. Parents can use a coaching approach when raising their children.

A coaching approach alludes to the possibility of using coaching skills and techniques without necessarily having a one-to-one conversation. Based on the three elements model presented in Chapter 2, the coaching approach can be understood as the 'skills' and 'way of being' elements, without the use of a coaching process. Essentially, we are talking about using some of the skills and approaches that we employ as coaches in other contexts and situations.

There are six things that you can start to do everyday, based on the skills and 'way of being' that you are developing as a coach:

- Listen to others.
- Allow for choices.
- Show an interest in others.
- Provide helpful feedback
- Believe in others.
- Encourage others to find meaningful goals.

Listen to others

Firstly, it is possible to adopt the 'power of listening' in everyday conversations, at home and in the workplace. If you are a parent, you may have been guilty of what might be called 'half-listening' to your children, especially if you are preoccupied with work-related matters or in the middle of doing something else. This can be changed straightaway, by providing quality listening time to children or family members when they have something to say. Even if this is not possible, it is preferable to postpone the conversation until you will be able to give others your full attention. At work, if you have gone into a conversation 'knowing' what the other party will say, you will have made it more difficult for yourself to genuinely listen.

Create time to listen to others

When people do talk to you, provide high-quality listening

Activity

PRACTICE: Next time a family member or close friend talks to you, try to implement the 20/80 rule. Allow the speaker 80% of the air time, and see whether this makes a difference.

Allow people choices

Secondly, allow people choices. We know that it is essential that coachees feel that they have choices. Researchers Deci and Ryan have found that this is necessary for human flourishing (1985). According to Self-Determination Theory (SDT), human beings need three things in order to flourish:

- They need to feel autonomous.
- They need to be part of human relationships.
- They need to know how well they are doing.

The feeling of autonomy is at the core of SDT. Through your behaviours, you can help others to feel autonomous. This can apply at home or in the workplace. The feeling of autonomy is not dependent on unlimited freedom or a total lack of any constraints. On the contrary, it is possible for autonomy to exist within a clear set of rules and boundaries. For example, for employees, whether or not they respond to customer inquiries will not be negotiable. However, how the individual staff member responds can be left as a choice for the employee. Parents may reasonably expect their child to study for upcoming exams, but how and when this is done could be left to the child. Forcing someone to do something and stipulating exactly how and when it must be done is likely to engender resistance. It is preferable, in a coaching approach, to agree and be explicit about a desired outcome, and then allow the person the autonomy to achieve this in a way that suits her. Choices can be created even when there is little flexibility. A parent could insist that a child wears a jacket before going out in the cold. Even then, the child could be presented with a choice of jackets.

Show an interest in others

Another element of SDT is the need for 'relatedness'. As stated earlier, human beings are social animals. We need differing levels of social interaction in order to feel positive about ourselves. So, at work, it is helpful to show an interest in others as human beings rather than simply professional colleagues. A small thing such as remembering a person's name can be very meaningful for an employee. When people encounter personal difficulties, a compassionate and empathic response is always appreciated. In times of personal distress, human kindness is most powerfully felt. In some societies, grief is awkward, and people often worry that they 'won't know what to say'. However, this can easily be interpreted as indifference. And a clumsy show of compassion is better than none at all. At work, remembering to ask about things that our colleagues are doing outside the workplace can provide evidence of interest in them as a human beings rather than just professional colleagues.

Provide helpful feedback

In coaching conversations, it may be easier to provide honest and direct feedback to the coachee. This is because the relationship is explicitly about supporting the coachee to achieve her goals and the coach's intentions are usually very obvious. Outside the coaching space, the provision of feedback is still valuable. Firstly, be generous with positive feedback. If someone does something well, or shows a positive side to her personality, let her know. We sometimes hold back from doing this, worrying that people will think that we are being patronising. Again, it is the intention that matters most of all. If you are being genuine and authentic about your feedback, it will usually be taken positively. And if you notice that something is holding a person back – perhaps the way she respond to emails, or how she dresses for certain work functions, think about whether that person would benefit from the information that you have. Remember, giving this type of feedback outside a coaching conversation is more risky. Before giving the feedback, make sure the person would like to hear it. Think about whether she is likely to be open to receiving this feedback from you. Be explicit about the reason that you are providing the feedback, tentative in the way you deliver it and clear that you are simply sharing your personal perceptions with her.

Believe in others

Believing in others is one of the foundations of the 'way of being' in coaches. Seminal research referenced earlier demonstrated how teachers' positive expectations could determine increases in pupils' IQ scores (Rosenthal and Jacobson, 1966). Called the 'self-fulfilling prophecy', Rosenthal and Jacobson showed that holding high expectations of others can lead to enhanced performance.

Encourage others to pursue meaningful goals

The pursuit of meaningful goals can lead to longer-lasting feelings of subjective well-being than actually achieving goals which are less meaningful (Hefferon and Boniwell, 2011). For this reason, it can be helpful to ask people to reflect on their goals, encouraging them to articulate what they are trying to achieve.

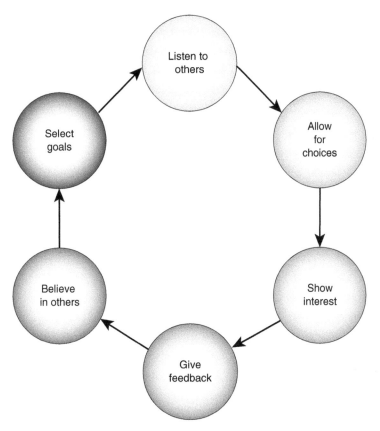

Figure 15.2   Six ways of adopting a 'way of being' all the time

To end this chapter, let us return to an activity that you completed at the very beginning of this book. In Chapter 2, we asked you to assess your level of confidence about coaching. It would be helpful if you did this again, without making reference to the earlier activity.

Activity

Take a moment to reflect on your current levels of confidence about coaching.

At this moment, how confident are you about your ability to coach? Draw a line with a '0' on one end and a '10' on the other. On this scale, select a number that represents your current level of confidence. Below the line, write down some of your thoughts about why you selected that number. For example, if you have said '6', what makes it a '6' and not a '0'?

Now look back at the earlier activity. Do you remember what you scored yourself initially? How has this changed?

PART SIX

CONCLUSION

16
REFLECTING ON PRACTICE

As we reach the final stage of this book, you should be feeling more confident about your ability to coach. I hope that the notion of 'becoming' a coach rather than learning *how* to coach has been made clearer. At this point, we have considered the skills of coaching, a well-known coaching process, some activities to encourage creativity and a 'way of being'. In this chapter, we return to explore something that has been implicit throughout the book: the need to be ethical and operate with integrity as a coach.

If you embrace what you have learned so far and choose to become a coach, you will, at times, be faced with 'ethical dilemmas' during your coaching conversations. We will start by discussing 'ethics' before outlining how we can be prepared for ethical dilemmas. The chapter will conclude by proposing ways of developing and maintaining our coaching practice in a way that is professional and ethical.

Ethics

What are 'ethics'? The Oxford Dictionary (www.oxforddictionaries.com) defines 'ethics' as 'moral principles that govern a person's behaviour or the conducting of an activity'. For our purposes, we can understand ethics as a set of principles and values that guides our coaching practice. Words such as 'good', 'bad', 'right' and 'wrong' are used when ethics are discussed. Our focus is on making the 'right' decisions during coaching conversations. As we will discover as we work through this chapter, this is not straightforward. The decision relating to the 'right' thing to do in a coaching conversation is dependent on a number of factors and will vary between coaches and situations.

Let us begin by considering some foundational ethical principles. In a survey of the ethical principles of a range of related professions, Brennan and Wildflower (2010) noted that there was broad consistency and the key points are listed below:

1. Do not cause harm to others.
2. Act in ways that promote the welfare of others.
3. Know the limits of your competence and work within these.
4. Respect the interests of the client.
5. Respect the law.

What is the situation with ethical codes of conduct for coaches?

Activity   Code of ethics

Go online and find a professional association for coaches that operates in your country. Find their website and locate their ethical code of conduct. This is usually freely available. Download or print this out for your reference. Once you have done this, go back online and see if you can find the codes of ethics of at least two other coaching associations from anywhere in the world. Highlight the ethical principles or guidelines that you can identify in all three documents.

Hopefully you will have been reassured to find that there are strong similarities between the various codes of ethics for coaches. I recommend that you select a professional association for coaching and apply to become a member. There are now a number of national and international associations for coaches. Firstly, being a member of such an association will build your professional credibility. Secondly, these associations can be useful sources of information and networking opportunities. Thirdly, they can provide you with links to coaching supervisors, group supervision sessions, training opportunities and other professional services for coaches. Most importantly, each professional association will have a code of ethics. It is essential that you **identify a code of ethics** to follow before you start to coach others.

Ethical moments of choice

As a coach, you will inevitably encounter 'ethical moments of choice' as part of your practice. In the coaching profession, these are usually referred to as 'ethical dilemmas' but this phrase is unhelpful and limiting. The word 'dilemma' suggests that these moments are always negative, and implies that there are usually only two ways to engage with them. By determining something to be an 'ethical dilemma', we are approaching a critically important moment in a coaching conversation from a negative position. I prefer to use of the phrase 'moment of choice', which I have adopted from Allard de Jong (2010). We shall use the term 'ethical moments of choice' to refer to instances when a coach is faced with an ethical question and must select one of a number of options to respond to it.

You may be curious about the kind of 'ethical moments of choice' that may arise during coaching conversations. A few genuine examples taken from supervisory conversations are listed below.

- The coachee seeks to exceed the agreed number of coaching sessions:
  The initial agreement between the coach and the coachee was for five sessions. In the last fifteen minutes of the fifth session, the coachee requests 'some more coaching' because she feels that there is still some 'unfinished business' to complete.

- The coach is offered additional work in a client's organisation:
  The initial agreement between the coach and the coachee was for six coaching sessions to support the executive's professional development. The coachee is so impressed with the coach that she now offers additional work delivering in-house training to staff in her organisation.
- The coach develops a physical attraction to the coachee:
  The coaching sessions are progressing well. Initially the coach notices that she looks forward to meeting the coachee more than is usual. At one point during a coaching conversation, she realises that her feelings towards the coachee are affected by a physical attraction.
- The coachee claims that she is being bullied:
  The coachee had requested coaching to discuss her relationship with colleagues at work. As this issue is explored, the coachee uses the word 'bullying' to describe how she is treated by a senior manager in the organisation.
- The coach cannot accept the moral position of the coachee:
  The coaching topic is about returning to work after maternity leave. During the third coaching session, the coachee makes a decision related to family planning that the coach cannot accept from a religious point of view.
- The coachee contravenes the principle of equal opportunity:
  The coach has been employed to support the coachee to implement a restructuring programme. During a coaching conversation, the coach discloses that she will ignore the correct recruitment process when offering a position to a colleague whose job is at risk.

Although it is easier to read about an ethical moment of choice here than engage with it during a coaching conversation, I hope that you found some of these scenarios challenging. Each is an ethical moment of choice for the coach. In this case, you are reading about ethical moments of choice without any pressure to respond to them straight away. As a reader, you have time to think about these carefully and none of your own values or principles is being directly tested. In coaching conversations, we do not have the luxury of this kind of thinking time as the ethical moments of choice are usually unexpected. As a coach, you would need to make a decision about how to respond. The section below proposes how to prepare for these ethical moments of choice.

1. Refer back to your coaching contract

In Chapter 7, the need for a coaching contract was discussed. Contracting should precede any coaching assignment. At a minimum, a coaching contract must include a shared understanding of what coaching entails, an explicit reference to the importance of confidentiality (including any exceptions to this), a mention of what will happen if the coachee divulges any information about illegal activity and what will happen if the coach feels that the discussion is moving towards an area which is outside her area of competence. Good practice would suggest that the contract should be comprehensive before the first session and then revisited briefly at the start of every coaching conversation. When faced with an ethical moment of choice, the first point of reflection should be **'what have we agreed in the coaching contract that relates to this situation?'** The need for a coaching contract cannot be over-emphasised. It forms the backbone of the coaching relationship and is critically important at ethical moments of choice.

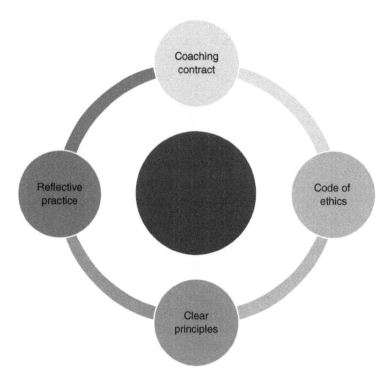

Figure 16.1   Information needed at ethical moments of choice

2. Identify a code of ethics

As I have already noted previously, it is essential to adopt a code of ethics. This is an important element of being prepared for ethical moments of choice. A necessary point of reflection is **'what does my code of ethics suggest about this situation?'** It may be good practice to keep a copy of the code of ethics with you. Some coaches share their code of ethics with their coachees and organisational clients.

3. Reflect on your own principles

Alongside the code of ethics, coaches must reflect on their own deeply-held values and principles. These are very personal to you. Each of us has values and a set of principles but few of us reflect on these explicitly. Doing so provides us with a moral compass that can guide us through ethical moments of choice. When coaching, our coachee's values and principles are also important. There may sometimes be a tension between the coachee's values and principles and yours. For this reason, decisions about ethical moments of choice should be taken after considering a number of different elements (contract, code of ethics, our own principles and previous experiences).

Deeply held beliefs   Activity

Identify about 30 minutes for this activity. Write down your deeply held beliefs and principles about what is right and what is wrong. If appropriate, do this in your learning journal. This is a valuable activity. It is very possible that some of the values and principles contradict one another. If this is the case, it is OK. However, I would invite you to regard this list as tentative. Once completed, this page of 'values and principles' can be used when reflecting on your coaching practice or during supervisory conversations.

4. Undertake reflective practice

As suggested throughout this book, coaches develop through practice and reflection. Based on the premise that we learn during every coaching session, it makes sense to capture this learning and think about how we can use any new information to enhance our coaching practice. There are essentially two practical ways of ensuring effective reflective practice: keeping a coaching journal and undertaking regular supervisory conversations.

SNAPSHOT   Responding to ethical moments of choice

1. Refer back to the **coaching contract.** What has been agreed with the coachee? Is there any reference to this situation?
2. Think about the **code of ethics** that you have adopted. What guidance can the code of ethics provide in this instance?
3. Consider your own deeply held **principles and values**. What should you do, based on your principles?
4. Take advantage of your **reflective practice.** Have you been in this type of situation before? How was this managed previously?

Coaching journal

A learning journal was recommended in the early part of this book. This is a very effective way of keeping a record of your learning. A coaching journal will provide a focus for your reflective practice and it is recommended that you add entries into it following every coaching session. Journal entries will provide you with a reminder of the coaching sessions and will form the basis of reflective practice.

Supervisory conversations

There is currently much discussion about the need for coaching supervision. According to the leading writers in this field (Hawkins and Smith, 2006), supervision is 'the process by which a coach with the help of a supervisor can attend to understanding better both the client system and themselves as part of the client–coach system, and by so doing transform their work and develop their craft' (p. 12). According to Hawkins and Smith, coaching supervision has three clear functions:

- Developmental: To develop the skills, understanding and capacities of the coach
- Resourcing: To attend to the emotions and well-being of the coach
- Qualitative: To ensure the quality of the coaching and adherence to ethical standards

The last point is what makes coaching supervision different from peer coaching. Coaching supervision has an evaluative, 'quality assurance' function, and the supervisor has a responsibility to the profession of coaching. Coaching supervisors tend to be experienced coaches or counsellors with training in supervision.

There is no doubt that coaches benefit from reflective conversations with more experienced colleagues as they continue to develop their practice. Different ways of accessing coaching supervision are listed below.

1. One-to-one supervision with a coach supervisor
   This is the most traditional way of accessing coaching supervision. The coach and her supervisor should meet regularly to talk about the coach's practice. Supervision sessions can last between one and two hours. The conversation focuses on the coach and her experiences, successes and challenges when coaching. This method is usually the most costly form of coaching supervision. Increasingly, telephone coaching supervision is available and represents a cost-effective alternative.
2. Group supervision facilitated by a coach supervisor
   This approach is growing in popularity within the field of coaching. In this way of working, a number of coaches attend regular supervision sessions with a coach supervisor. These sessions are of varying length, depending on the number of coaches involved. The focus of the conversation remains on the experiences, success and challenges of the participating coaches (supervisees). Not every coach will necessarily have the chance to share her own experiences at every session. However, there are opportunities for learning from one another's experiences. Group supervision is usually more cost effective than one-to-one supervision.
3. Facilitated peer supervision in groups
   Some groups of coaches have developed internally managed peer supervision groups. In this format, every member of the group adopts the position of peer supervisor. One member of the group takes the role of facilitator, and manages the coaching supervision process so that everyone involved has a chance to support the coach (supervisee) as she shares her experiences with the group. Again, participants can support one another and learn from other coaches' experiences. All members of the facilitated peer supervision group would require some training in coaching supervision.
4. Supervisory conversations with an experienced coach
   Less formal, but still helpful are agreed supervisory conversations organised on an ad-hoc basis with an experienced coach. These can take place in person or over the telephone. As needed, the

coach will contact the more experienced coach if there are coaching-related topics that she would like to discuss.

5. Peer supervision

   Some coaches have arranged peer supervision in pairs, working with a coach with whom they have a good relationship. Peer supervision can take place regularly, with coaches taking turns to bring topics to the conversation or splitting the time equally so that both parties can receive supervisory support.

SNAPSHOT   What level of coaching supervision is required?

To some extent, this is a personal decision. Every coach must create structured opportunities to reflect on her practice. Table 16.1 is only a recommendation. Different approaches will suit different coaches.

SNAPSHOT   What topics should be brought to supervisory conversations?

Good practice in this field would suggest that it is helpful for coaches to take at least 15 minutes of reflection time prior to the coaching session and a similar amount of time at the end of a coaching session. Supervision exists to support the coach to explore or resolve any questions, concerns or doubts that emerge from coaching. So, as a general rule, if there is something niggling away at your mind following a coaching session, this is the best indication that this topic should be taken to a supervisory conversation. Resolving this type of concern quickly is an important part of the coach's well-being and represents good professional practice.

Table 16.1 Suggested ways of accessing supervision

Role	Supervisory arrangements
People who coach professionally and frequently	One-to-one supervision with a coach supervisor
People who coach professionally but infrequently	One-to-one supervision with a coach supervisor or group supervision facilitated by a coach supervisor
People learning how to coach	Group supervision facilitated by a coach supervisor or facilitated peer supervision in groups
People working in organisations who coach others as a secondary role	Group supervision facilitated by a coach supervisor or facilitated peer supervision in groups
People who manage others using a 'coaching approach'	Peer supervision if needed
People with significant experience of coaching who coach infrequently	Supervision arrangements may include all of the suggested options

Activity   Your ethical practice

Write at least one paragraph in your learning journal explaining how you will ensure that you practice ethically and professionally as a coach.

Developing ethical maturity

Ethical maturity is developed through reflective practice and coaching experience. It has been proposed that ethical maturity can be 'enhanced by engaging in regular supervision in which hypothetical testing of dilemmas can be utilised, by recurrent ethical thinking, engaging in activities associated with coach training and pursuing wider continual professional development' (Duffy and Passmore, 2010).

Based on the discussion on this chapter, I would like to propose the virtuous cycle of ethical maturity. Following this cycle will provide a structured process for developing ethical maturity in coaches.

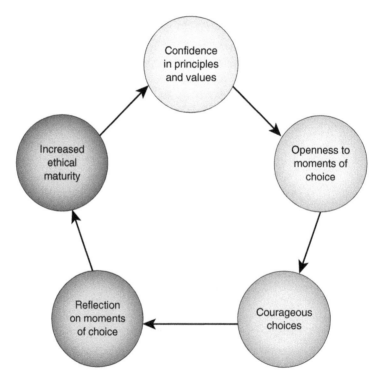

Figure 16.2   Virtuous cycle of ethical maturity

Reflect back on the principles and values that you noted in your learning journal earlier in this chapter. Building your confidence in these (alongside effective contracting and adherence to an ethical code) will allow you to approach ethical moments of choice with a more positive and open attitude. If you respond with such an attitude, you are likely to make courageous choices. In other words, you will not avoid or ignore the ethical moment of choice. You will be able to see it as a critical moment in the coaching conversation and address it in a way that respects the coachee and is ethically justifiable. Your courageous choices should be reflected upon and discussed during supervision. This will allow you (and others) to celebrate and learn from ethical moments of choice and therefore develop your ethical maturity. Increased ethical maturity will build confidence in your principles and values. And the virtuous circle continues!

Continuing professional development of coaches

As we have reached the end of this part of your learning journey, you will need to start considering how to continue to develop yourself professionally. Due to the current global interest in coaching, there are many providers of coaching training in the UK, the USA, Australia, Europe and internationally. These range from very short courses provided by commercial training organisations to in-house coach training programmes delivered within large corporations to postgraduate coaching programmes at universities.

It is now possible to study for a masters in coaching psychology at university and even to complete professional doctorates or PhDs on the topic of coaching. Each coach is best placed to identify what will be most helpful for her own professional development. For some, a certificate or university qualification will provide credibility and an endorsement of their skills. Others will be interested in broadening their 'toolbox' of approaches and techniques by attending short courses and seminars on specialist topics such as cognitive-behavioural therapy, mindfulness or the use of psychometrics.

Conclusion

I hope that this introductory text has provided you with a foundation for your practice but also a curiosity and desire to continually develop as a coach. Firstly, if you have not done so already, you may want to find a coach for yourself. If we believe that coaching is beneficial and potentially life-changing, we should have coaches ourselves. Secondly, find ways of connecting with other coaches. We learn best together and coaches should be collaborative, positive people. Finally, identify the right supervisory arrangement that will support you as you coach others.

Activity   Time to reflect

Now is a good time to reflect on your own learning journey as you have engaged with this text, the activities and video clips. If you were to select one piece of personal learning that you would highlight above any other, what would it be? Take your time to write one sentence that captures this. If you would like to share this, please do so by visiting the Companion Website (**www.sagepub.co.uk/vannieuwerburgh**). Your insight is likely to inspire others.

If you are still a little bit anxious about coaching others, this is wonderful news. This anxiety is something that should be kept alive and part of your coaching practice. Being anxious about a coaching session is an indication that you want to get it right for your coachee. A reasonable level of anxiety also allows us to remain humble, interested and present during coaching conversations. The challenge is to get just the right level of anxiety! And the best way to get the balance right is to coach, coach and coach.

As you become more experienced, you will notice that you are starting to automatically and naturally integrate the three elements of coaching. The skills will start to feel natural, the process will melt into the background and your 'way of being' will infuse and enhance the coaching relationship (see Figure 16.3). Enjoy the process of becoming a coach – it never ends! Finally, watch Video 16.2 for some concluding thoughts and a coaching question.

Figure 16.3   Way of being

REFERENCES

Alexander, G. (2010) 'Behavioural coaching – the GROW model', in J. Passmore (ed.), *Excellence in Coaching: The Industry Guide*, 2nd edn. London: Kogan Page. pp. 83–93.

Alexander, G. and Renshaw, B. (2005) *Supercoaching: The Missing Ingredient for High Performance*. London: Random House.

Banyard, P.E., Davies, M.N.O., Norman, C. and Winder, B. (eds) (2010) *Essential Psychology: A Concise Introduction*. London: Sage.

Boniwell, I. (2012) *Positive Psychology in a Nutshell: The Science of Happiness*, 3rd edn. Maidenhead: Open University Press.

Brennan, D. and Wildflower, L. (2010) 'Ethics in coaching', in E. Cox, T. Bachkirova and D. Clutterbuck (eds), *The Complete Handbook of Coaching*. London: Sage. pp. 369–80.

Bresser, F. and Wilson, C. (2010) 'What is coaching?', in J. Passmore (ed.), *Excellence in Coaching: The Industry Guide*, 2nd edn. London: Kogan Page. pp. 9–26.

Brock, V.G. (2012) *Sourcebook of Coaching History*. Self-published.

Brown, P. and Brown, V. (2012) *Neuropsychology for Coaches: Understanding the Basics*. Maidenhead: Open University Press.

Buzan, T. (2002) *How to Mind Map*. London: Thorsons.

Cox, E., Bachkirova, T. and Clutterbuck, D. (eds) (2010) *The Complete Handbook of Coaching*. London: Sage.

de Haan, E. (2008a) 'I struggle and emerge: critical moments of experienced coaches', *Consulting Psychology Journal: Practice and Research*, 60 (1): 106–31.

de Haan, E. (2008b) *Relational Coaching: Journeys towards Mastering One to One Learning*. Chichester: Wiley.

de Haan, E., Bertie, C., Day, A. and Sills, C. (2010) 'Critical moments of clients and coaches: a direct-comparison study', *International Coaching Psychology Review*, 5 (2): 109–28.

de Jong, A. (2010) 'Coaching ethics: integrity in the moment of choice', in J. Passmore (ed.), *Excellence in Coaching: The Industry Guide*, 2nd edn. London: Kogan Page. pp. 204–14.

De Lozier, J. and Grinder, J. (1987) *Turtles All the Way Down: Prerequisites to Personal Genius.* Bonny Doon, CA: Grinder, DeLozier and Associates.

de Shazer, S. and Berg, I.K. (1995) 'The brief therapy tradition', in J. Weakland and W. Ray (eds), *Propagations: Thirty Years of Influence from the Mental Research Institute.* Binghamton, NY: Haworth Press. pp. 249–52.

Deci, E. L. and Ryan, R. M. (1985) *Intrinsic Motivation and Self-Determination in Human Behaviour.* New York: Plenum.

Deci, E.L. and Ryan, R.M. (eds) (2002) *Handbook of Self-Determination Research.* Rochester, NY: University of Rochester Press.

Downey, M. (2003) *Effective Coaching: Lessons from the Coach's Coach,* 2nd edn. London: Texere.

Duffy, M. and Passmore, J. (2010) 'Ethics in coaching: an ethical decision making framework for coaching psychologists', *International Coaching Psychology Review,* 5 (2): 140–51.

Frederickson, B. and Losada, M. (2005) 'Positive affect and the complex dynamics of human flourishing', *American Psychologist,* 60 (7): 678–86.

Gallwey, W.T. (1974) *The Inner Game of Tennis.* New York: Random House.

Garvey, R., Stokes, P. and Megginson, D. (2009) *Coaching and Mentoring: Theory and Practice.* London: Sage.

Goleman, D. (1996) *Emotional Intelligence: Why it Matters More than IQ.* New York: Bantam.

Grant, A.M. (2003) 'The impact of life coaching on goal attainment, metacognition, and mental health', *Social Behavior and Personality,* 31 (3): 253–64.

Grant, A.M. (2012) 'An integrated model of goal-focused coaching: an evidence-based framework for teaching and practice', *International Coaching Psychology Review,* 7 (2): 146–65.

Grencavage, L. and Norcross, J. (1990) 'Where are the commonalities among the therapeutic common factors?', *Professional Psychology: Research and Practice,* 21 (5): 372–78.

Hawkins, P. and Smith, N. (2006) *Coaching, Mentoring and Organizational Consultancy: Supervision and Development.* London: McGraw-Hill.

Hefferon, K. and Boniwell, I. (2011) *Positive Psychology: Theory, Research and Applications.* Maidenhead: Open University Press.

Iyengar, S. (2010) *The Art of Choosing.* New York: Twelve.

Kauffman, C. (2006) 'Positive psychology: The science at the heart of coaching', in D. R. Stober and A. M. Grant (eds), *Evidence Based Coaching Handbook: Putting Best Practices to Work for Your Clients.* Hoboken, NJ: John Wiley. pp. 219–53.

Kline, N. (1999) *Time to Think: Listening to Ignite the Human Mind.* London: Cassell.

Knight, J. (2011) *Unmistakable Impact: A Partnership Approach for Dramatically Improving Instruction.* Thousand Oaks, CA: Corwin.

Locke, E.A. (1996) 'Motivation through conscious goal setting', *Applied and Preventative Psychology,* 5 (2): 117–24.

Locke, E.A. and Latham, G.P. (2002) 'Building a practically useful theory of goal setting and task motivation', *American Psychologist,* 57 (9): 705–17.

Losada, M. and Heaphy, E. (2004) 'The role of positivity and connectivity in the performance of business teams: a nonlinear dynamics model', *American Behavioural Scientist,* 47 (6): 740–65.

McKenna, D.D. and Davis, S.L. (2009) 'Hidden in plain sight: the active ingredients of executive coaching', *Industrial and Organizational Psychology*, 2: 244–60.

Orem, S.L., Binkert, J. and Clancy, A.L. (2007) *Appreciative Coaching: A Positive Process for Change*. San Francisco, CA: Jossey-Bass.

Palmer, S. and Szymanska, K. (2007) 'Cognitive behavioural coaching: an integrative approach', in S. Palmer and A. Whybrow (eds), *Handbook of Coaching Psychology: A Guide for Practitioners*. London: Routledge. pp. 86–117.

Passmore, J. (2007) 'Behavioural coaching', in S. Palmer and A. Whybrow (eds), *Handbook of Coaching Psychology: A Guide for Practitioners*. London: Routledge. pp. 73–85.

Passmore, J. (ed) (2010) *Excellence in Coaching: The Industry Guide*, 2nd edn. London: Kogan Page.

Pease, A. and Pease, B. (2005) *The Definitive Book of Body Language*. London: Orion.

Peltier, B. (2010) *The Psychology of Executive Coaching: Theory and Application*, 2nd edn. London: Routledge.

Raia, A.P. (1965) 'Goal setting and self-control: an empirical study', *Journal of Management Studies*, 2 (1): 34–53.

Rogers, C.R. (1957) 'The necessary and sufficient conditions of therapeutic personality change', *Journal of Consulting Psychology*, 21: 95–103.

Rogers, C.R. (1980) *A Way of Being*. Boston, MA: Houghton Mifflin.

Rosenthal, R. and Jacobson, L. (1966) 'Teachers' expectancies: Determinants of pupils' IQ gains', *Psychological Reports*, 19: 115–18.

Rosenthal, R. and Jacobson, L. (1968) *Pygmalion in the Classroom: Teacher Expectation and Pupils' Intellectual Development*. Norwalk, CT: Crown House.

Salovey, P. and Mayer, J. (1990) 'Emotional intelligence', *Imagination, Cognition, and Personality*, 9 (3): 185–211.

Schwartz, B. (2004) *The Paradox of Choice: Why More is Less*. New York: Harper Perennial.

Thomson, B. (2012) *With No Attachment to the Answer: Non-Directive Coaching: Attitudes, Approaches and Applications*. Nottingham: Nottingham University Press.

van Nieuwerburgh, C. (ed.) (2012) *Coaching in Education: Getting Better Results for Students, Educators, and Parents*. London: Karnac.

van Nieuwerburgh, C., and Tong, C. (2013) 'Exploring the benefits of being a student coach in educational settings: a mixed methods study', *Coaching: An International Journal of Theory, Practice and Research*, 6 (1): 5–24.

Whitmore, J. (1992) *Coaching for Performance: A Practical Guide to Growing Your Own Skills*. London: Nicholas Brealey.

Whitmore, J. (2009) *Coaching for Performance: GROWing Human Potential and Purpose: The Principles and Practice of Coaching and Leadership*, 4th edn. London: Nicholas Brealey.

Willis, P. (2005) '*EMCC competency research project: Phase 2*', Watford: European Mentoring and Coaching Council.

INDEX